Also by Donna Tiernan Mahoney:

Touching the Face of God,

published by Jeremiah Press,
Boca Raton, Florida, 1990 & Mercier Press,
Cork and Dublin, Ireland, 1991.

SEDUCED BY GORGONZOLA

Reflections of a
Reluctant Restaurateur

*Evelyn & Bob,
Hope some of our crazy restaurant stories will bring a smile to your faces!*

Donna Tiernan Mahoney

Blessings, Donna

Copyright © 2015 Donna Mahoney.

All rights reserved. No part of this book may be reproduced, stored, or transmitted by any means—whether auditory, graphic, mechanical, or electronic—without written permission of both publisher and author, except in the case of brief excerpts used in critical articles and reviews. Unauthorized reproduction of any part of this work is illegal and is punishable by law.

ISBN: 978-1-4834-4064-4 (sc)
ISBN: 978-1-4834-4066-8 (hc)
ISBN: 978-1-4834-4065-1 (e)

Library of Congress Control Number: 2015918060

Because of the dynamic nature of the Internet, any web addresses or links contained in this book may have changed since publication and may no longer be valid. The views expressed in this work are solely those of the author and do not necessarily reflect the views of the publisher, and the publisher hereby disclaims any responsibility for them.

Manero's Is a registered name used with the permission of the owners of Manero's LLC. Any reproduction or use of the name or logo for any commercial purpose is strictly prohibited.

Any people depicted in stock imagery provided by Thinkstock are models, and such images are being used for illustrative purposes only. Certain stock imagery © Thinkstock.

Lulu Publishing Services rev. date: 11/18/2015

CONTENTS

Dedication ix
In Gratitude xiii
Foreword xv
Preface xix
Introduction 1
Chapter 1   Our Mainiero Family and Manero's in Greenwich 3
Chapter 2   Manero's in Hallandale, Florida 28
Chapter 3   Manero's in West Palm Beach, Florida 68
Chapter 4   J. Arthur's in Maggie Valley, North Carolina 104
Chapter 5   Manero's in Palm City, Florida 143
Chapter 6   Pilgrimage to Gorgonzola 178
Restaurant Information 191
The Manero Family Tree 195
The Tiernan Family Tree 196
Acknowledgments 197

In loving memory of John Maher Mahoney, Jr.

DEDICATION

Over the years we have made so many dear and lifelong friends as a result of our interactions with them in our restaurants. At first, these people were our guests, then friends, then lifelong confidants. Because of them, our lives have been extremely meaningful and blessed. You know who you are and to all of you I dedicate this book, *Seduced by Gorgonzola*.

...And to our children, Jay and Marcy, Rick and Michelle, Shannon and John, Erin, and grandchildren, John Patrick, Jake, Reilly, Lillie, Matthew, Keagan, Isabella, and Ella with whom the Manero legacy rests.

And the end to all our exploring will be to arrive where we started and know the place for the first time.

—T. S. Eliot

IN GRATITUDE

The restaurant business has been very good to our family. I thank our Creator for it each day.

This business has given us lives filled with challenge, creativity, adventure, meaning, and very few dull moments.

On any given day, this business drains every ounce of our energy and challenges us to the max. It has great promise one day and great disappointment the next. It brings excitement and constant worry into our lives. In good times and bad, it has provided the means for us to raise our families and to understand the depth and beauty of life.

The restaurant has provided our families and our colleagues the means to a variety of educational opportunities. It has enabled us to be fully integrated into every level of society, to provide hospitality, to help those in need, to celebrate lives, to counsel and be counseled. It has brought us in contact with the prince and the pauper, the businessperson, the immigrant, the sportsperson, the politician, the ex-convict, and the religious and to recognize the nobility and humanity in all of them, as well as in ourselves.

It is this business, this wild, crazy, sometimes insufferable business, and all those who have brought us to where we are today for which and for whom we are extremely grateful.

FOREWORD

It was nearly forty years ago, I was riding shotgun in her station wagon when Donna Tiernan Mahoney Lynch first came into my life. After some initial pleasantries, she informed me that if I was not prepared to fully embrace a weekly grouping of women after a church-sponsored Cursillo, I should not bother attending the Cursillo (a Christian renewal weekend) at all.

Harrumph. This was a different breed of cat. No attempt to beguile me into attending a full weekend of singing, sharing, listening, and so on. I was intrigued by this person. Four decades later, I remain intrigued. Having the honor of a ringside seat in her grand play, I would like to introduce you to the star — the author of this delightful memoir.

Donna Tiernan graduated with a degree in psychology from Manhattanville College for women in the late sixties. She was schooled, fashioned, encouraged, and when necessary, commanded (some might suggest brainwashed) to become…a wife, a mother, a pillar of her community, a bastion of her parish church. In the process, she dressed well, socially promoted her husband, joined the Junior League, volunteered at school, provided a children's taxi service, was a tutorial resource. And, of course, above all exemplified a lady.

Donna Tiernan married John Maher Mahoney and became Donna Tiernan Mahoney in a storybook wedding and they happily produced four beautiful children in the following eight years. The Mahoney children all turned out well, each one smart, dedicated, and above all, caring. In the course of raising this handful, Donna and John lived life large and small. She and John owned Manero's in West Palm Beach for many years. Their restaurant was a West Palm mainstay...*the* place to celebrate everything from pregnancies both planned and unplanned, graduations, engagements, birthdays, promotions; even deaths and firings required a Donna/John /Manero steak, onion rings, and above all, a Gorgonzola cheese salad. Their love, hilarity, and hospitality oversaw the milestones of multiple generations.

In the process, Donna returned to graduate school at the regional seminary for a degree in theology. Interesting: our "Donna Reed" lost her childlike faith and "found God"; wrote a book, "*Touching the Face of God*"; served as chair of the Board of Directors for Catholic Charities, President of our Council Catholic of Women, and then as National Vice President and a National Chair for that same organization. Donna engaged in every sport playable by either boy or girl. She loved, entertained, and drove John crazy; often in the reverse order...much to the entertainment of themselves and everyone else.

By the mid-nineties, with kids in college and graduate school, John and Donna decided to move the restaurant to Palm City and kick back a bit. No sooner had they sold the property than John was diagnosed with cancer. Bad cancer. While reeling with fear, Donna became his personal health advocate. She learned more about holistic medicine, cancer diets, focused therapy, and centering prayer in one week than many professionals, most gurus, and any monk ever learn. Shepherding their kids, she carried John and dragged us through the entire experience. She refused to give up, until finally, climbing into his hospital bed, she literally gave him back to God.

John's funeral was the most spirit filled and holy event most of us had ever attended. Oxymoronic or not, it was also the social event of the season. Everyone who attended John's Mass was invited to dinner served in the Mahoney enormous backyard on tables fully set with linen and silver and featuring their world famous Gorgonzola cheese salad. Both sides of the dualism created, orchestrated, and directed by...you guessed it.

Years of grief and bereavement followed, but they were years filled with growth and determined energy to survive and thrive. Their kids each married, interestingly all four of the marriages were to persons who had also lost a parent to death.

More than eight years after John's death and after much discernment, Donna and a very close priest friend took a remarkable leap of faith into a new life for both of them — a life together. Tim who had been the Vicar for Marriage and the Family in the Diocese of Palm Beach decided to try the very lifestyle in which he directed and encouraged others. They have been married for nine years now and would agree that decision was divinely inspired.

So, who is this "different breed of cat"? The little girl who grew up over a restaurant dreaming of a big backyard, the beloved daughter of a professional golfer turned restaurateur and a Manero Mom, the sister of a successful lawyer/writer, the rule-following Catholic schoolgirl, the successful suburbanite with grand parties and entertaining, the thinking nonconformist, the world traveling adventurer, a published author, a doctor of ministry all whilst being and maintaining the priority of family.

She is a woman who didn't like to cook, who did not want to be involved with restaurants, who is now the matriarch of the Manero's Group, a woman who wanted to practice psychology, who relishes joy but can weep with abandon. She is a woman who, with Tim, takes folks on storytelling tours of Ireland, who is now telling her story. She calls it her journey. I think you will enjoy the trip.

— Marnie Ritchie Poncy, Esq.; RN.

PREFACE

This book is a story about the Manero family as seen through my eyes. It details some of the humorous and meaningful life lessons that we have learned through almost eighty years of the business in which our family has been engaged. The reader will note that the first chapter is historical and as the chapters move on, the genre becomes more one of stories, all of which are born from real-life experiences.

I write this book to honor all the generations of those who have made our family restaurants successful and the hub of hospitality that they have been for many. Over the years, literally, thousands of people have recounted to me stories of early and recent years and the fun times they have had in one or more of our family's restaurants. Some of these were just too good to be forgotten.

A writer's task is to convey a message. All information shared here is true to the best of my memories and those of family members and friends named in the acknowledgments in the back of this book. In addition, I have used a variety of local and state records, archives, newspaper articles, and magazines to write this book, especially the first chapter. I have tried to verify information to the best of my ability. In doing so, I found several articles to contain conflicting dates and relationships that I knew to be incorrect. I have tried to confirm the correct ones and bring them to light when historical documentation was available.

When it was not problematic, embarrassing, or contrary to desires of friends and guests, real names have been used. The time frames to the best of my knowledge, are accurate, formulated from historical documents as well as books cited in the endnotes, newspaper articles, pictures, conversations, memories, and the like.

In order to honor and respect our guests and employees, each one of whom was a blessing to us in some way, I have changed some names, situations, and time frames to protect their anonymity. When a name, situation, and/or time frame has been altered, the reader can recognize it as a name will be written in italics the first time someone is mentioned in a story.

Gorgonzola is a veined Italian blue cheese made from unskimmed cow's milk. It can be buttery and firm or crumbly. (Wikipedia)

Clydesdale horses, circa 1953.
Clydesdale horses used with permission of Anheuser-Busch, LLC. All rights reserved.

INTRODUCTION

Vivid in my memory is the spring morning those eight magnificent Clydesdales clattered down Steamboat Road and posed right in front of my grandmother's home in Greenwich, Connecticut. It was early in the 1950s and people had come from all over the state and surrounding New York towns to see the Anheuser-Busch wagon with all of its glitter and spectacle. The aura of fantasy and the excitement in the crowds of young and old made the blood rush through my small body.

Riveted to the scene, my eyes just about popped out of my five-year-old head. It was like a carnival, and wonder of all, it was my family, the Maneros, who were at the center of it. The horses had come that day as a part of a promotional deal sponsored by Anheuser-Busch. My Uncle Nick's first restaurant had become well known in the northeast at that point. Manero's Steak House was promoting Anheuser-Busch and in turn, because of the restaurant's increasing popularity, Anheuser-Busch was helping to promote the popular restaurant in Greenwich Harbor.

Feelings of pride swelled up in me. There was no other place or no other people in the world with whom I would want to be. The same childlike excitement and dazzling vision of that day has remained with me ever since. Flashing forward over sixty years, I have come to see the magic in a fuller and brighter light. My years as a part of the Manero family and my work in the family business has been more than magic. Through good times and challenging ones I have lived and continued the Manero legacy and have been divinely blessed in doing so.

The blessings have come from God, our Energy Source, Whom none of us can fully grasp. The blessings have come by way of my late husband, John, our children, and theirs, through my parents, brother, and sister-in law, through aunts, uncles, cousins, nieces, nephews, in-laws, and outlaws. The blessings have come by way of the thousands of employees who have signed their W-4s under some of the twenty-odd businesses our extended restaurant family has operated. And finally, the blessings have come from the literally millions of customers who have dined within our walls. They share our story.

The only question in life is whether or not you are going to answer a hearty "yes" to your adventure.
—Joseph Campbell

CHAPTER ONE

Our Mainiero Family and Manero's in Greenwich

The Beginnings in Greenwich

My grandparents, Giovanni and Maria Grazia Mainiero, were Italian immigrants who came to this country around the turn of the last century. They emigrated from Castelfranco in the province of Benevento, Italy. My grandfather came first, sometime after 1896. My grandmother, for whom I am named (Donna Grace Marie), followed around 1900 with my Aunt Mary, age four. Neither of my grandparents spoke English and my recollection of my grandma, when she died in 1954, was that she still spoke very little English. They settled in a poor Italian community living on Mulberry Street in the Bronx, where things were difficult for a young family who had come seeking a better life. After a series of illnesses, Grandpa was told to move Grandma out of the area because of the poor air quality, caused by the sewage flowing in the streets, which was negatively impacting her health. Around 1904, they moved to Rye, New York, where they lived for a few years before they moved to Railroad and Davis Avenues in Greenwich, Connecticut.

Mulberry Street, Bronx, early 1900s.

Even at the time my grandparents settled in the Greenwich area, it was one of the most upscale areas of the country. How they came to choose this area has always puzzled me. I can only imagine that it must have been more than a little challenging for them to integrate into American society. However, there was an opportunity for my grandfather to use his craft of shoemaking in the wealthy town (not to mention the profiting from gallons of his homemade wine, sold to his cronies from his garage). In addition, there was the added benefit of living with my grandmother's sister's family, Josephine and Pasquale Schinto. Not speaking the language, there was strength and comfort in being with family and security in larger numbers.

Grandma was a gentle but strong woman, two qualities necessary to raise large families in those difficult times. She birthed nine children; one died soon after he was born and another, Jackie, her youngest son and favorite, died in an accident. Grandma provided the means, encouragement, and confidence for education and skills for her family.

I knew little about my grandfather, Giovanni, as he died of a ruptured appendix in his late fifties. In the 1930s, medicine was not as advanced as it is now, so his critical condition became fatal. I have been told that he was a difficult and sometimes violent man. I suspected by my mother's occasional mention of him that he suffered from an undiagnosed mental illness. My mother was petrified of him. When she was a young child, he would intimidate and threaten the family with his gun. As a result, my mother had nightmares about the situation until the day she died. Often the two oldest sons, Nick and Clarence (Porky), would protect my grandmother and the family when Giovanni was abusive. His drinking continued until after the death of their son, Jackie, of whom, ironically, my grandfather was jealous. It was at that point that my grandfather, consumed by guilt, stopped his drinking and never took a drop of alcohol again. Unfortunately though, he lived only a few years after this change of behavior and heart.

On April 29, 1911, while my grandmother was newly pregnant with my mom, Ellen, she and my grandfather went about purchasing the property at 557 Greenwich Avenue (which later became Steamboat Road) in Grandma's name. Ironically, Grandma purchased it from James Stubbs. Mr. Stubbs was the grandfather of Ginny Costaregni who would, years later, become Grandma's grandson's wife. (Ginny married Maria Grace's grandson, my first cousin, John Costaregni.) Another irony was that Ginny's grandfather, James Stubbs, also sold property in 1911 to Jimmy and Johnny Maher, great uncles of John Maher Mahoney, Jr. who, years later, would become my husband. They built a huge business called Maher Brothers also on Steamboat Road in Greenwich. (If you are not still with me after this paragraph, see family genealogies in the rear of book for clarifications about family members.)

Grandma was in her early thirties when she purchased the property. It consisted of 52½ feet on the famous Steamboat Road in Greenwich. There must have been a reason that the property was in her name. This would have been unusual, especially in an Italian family, typically male dominant in business issues. It was here that she and my grandfather opened a grocery store and lived on the property with their expanding family. The grocery store was below their residence (as was typical in the old country) and supported their family of eight children for many years. Most of the children worked part time there during their schooling. In the beginning, life was difficult, but as the children got older things improved. By the time most of them were twelve they had small jobs and their labor began to produce results as the store flourished. For an Italian immigrant family, things were getting better and better and the family grew up in a middle-class lifestyle for about a decade of their lives. As a result, the eldest son of these poor Italian immigrants, my Uncle Nick, was sent to college and then to law school to pursue his dream.

The Mainiero Family, circa 1922.

In 1927, not long before the Depression decimated the economy, life hit bottom for my mom's family as her brother, Jackie, died of a broken neck as a result of a tragic diving accident on Island Beach in Greenwich. The family was engulfed in sorrow and grief as they tried to process this terrible death of my grandmother's favorite son. Grandma was devastated. I was always of the impression that she never fully recovered from the grief of his death.

Then in 1929 came the Depression. As a result of this, Grandma could see that business was dropping off and the large yachts from which many of her customers came began disappearing. Pursers were fired and had to find other means of employment so they were no longer shopping at the store. The grocery store closed for a time as money got tight, even for the wealthy customers from the boatyard across the street. My grandfather had been working for the local Maher Brothers Mill (John's uncles, previously mentioned) by this time. These times were difficult for the whole country. Some of the children were forced to leave school and go to work. It would have been unthinkable to turn your head if your family needed help. Several of them, including my mother, got outside jobs to help their family survive.

By the mid-thirties, Grandpa had died and Grandma's children were grown. Some were married and many still lived in the apartments above the restaurant. Although the Depression still had deleterious effects all across the country, my Uncle Clarence (nicknamed Porky, sometimes spelled Porkie) who was the second oldest son, decided to open a small restaurant, The 19th Hole, in a part of the grocery store, where the butcher store later came to be. Porky, by this time, was a professional golfer and was well known in the Greenwich/Westchester area. He had come up through the ranks, first working as a caddy at the Greenwich Country Club. Apparently he was quite good, as at least two newspaper articles in my family's collection mentioned that he was the youngest qualifier in the National Open Golf Tournament in 1926 at Baltusrol Country Club. He apparently made this decision to open The 19th Hole, in part, as a result of the repeal of Prohibition, which took place on December 5, 1933. Taking advantage of this situation, it was only a month after, that Uncle Porky opened his business, described by some as a nightclub, on January 4, 1934. Records provided by the Greenwich Historical Society show Clarence Mainiero as the proprietor of this business from 1934 through 1941.[1] This would have been a bold move on his part as the whole country was deep into the Depression at this time, but apparently it was less severe in this wealthy area of the country. According to my eldest living family member, George Costaregni, at some stage the place was run by both Porky and Nick.

Family albums show that there must have been some family squabbles between the two of them as the invitation below seems to indicate.

Invitation to the opening of Uncle Porkie's 19th Hole, date handwritten by my father.

Many articles written about Uncle Nick indicated that he worked as a law clerk for the renowned Mayor Fiorello La Guardia of New York City, so perhaps he was working in the city during at least some of this time. By the late 1930s, the new venture, in spite of the Depression, was running well and had become a popular place for people to gather. Uncle Porky attracted many of his golfing friends to the business. Uncle Nick was an excellent golfer as well. More importantly, however, Tony Manero had long before this time married my Aunt Agnes. Tony was not a direct relative, although many newspaper articles state that he was. Tony (a pro at Sedgefield Country Club in Greensboro, NC from 1933-1937)[2] had won the 1936 U.S. Open and had also played on the Ryder Cup team and when not touring, he was often seen on the property. Many great golfing photos appear on the internet of Tony, sometimes along with other famous golfers of the age. One can imagine he was a real draw for people frequenting The 19th Hole.

Uncle Tony and Aunt Agnes Manero
(with Grandma Mainiero in the background)
Prior to their marriage and to his winning of the
1936 U.S. Open Golf Championship.

The location of the business in a lovely area of Greenwich, not far from the Connecticut /New York State line, made it convenient for many to drop in after a game of golf. Ironically, my Uncle Tony (not only a champion golfer but a delightful man) never drank, but his presence at the bar and grill or nightclub/restaurant (there are many different family accounts on this) was a big plus for the small family business which was quickly becoming quite sustaining. In addition, as the economy improved, many of the wealthy boaters again docked across the street at the Island Beach docks, and would stop in for a sandwich and glass of beer after disembarking their boats.

As the effects of the Depression began to wear off, the grocery store was reopened. According to information gleaned from my Aunt Mary Margenot (eldest daughter in the Mainiero family) in an interview done by the Greenwich Library Oral History Project,[3] the Depression wasn't as difficult in Greenwich as it was in the rest of the country. I'm sure the market in which they were dealing was what made the difference. When both the businesses became more prosperous, they expanded, again catering on an even larger scale to the large luxury boats which would dock across the street on Steamboat Road. In addition, my grandmother took in boarders and mentored many young people in the American way of life. Taking in boarders was not uncommon in those times. These were mostly young Italian immigrants who would live in Grandma's apartments for short periods of time. For a woman who spoke almost no English, except what she learned from her eldest daughter, my Aunt Mary, and her children as they grew up, she was extremely entrepreneurial. It seemed that although she seldom spoke, she understood the English language and our American culture remarkably well.

Enter my dad, Art Tiernan, who had grown up comfortably before the Crash but who was, at the time, not the least bit wealthy. He was a superb golfer who turned pro at an early age. He was one of those who would come in off the boats from Bermuda and need somewhere to wet his whistle. He was working on the boats as a steward. It was normal for him to stop in for a drink, search out a foursome for a game of golf at one of the local clubs, and then take off for a day at the golf club. He did this when the boat docked in Greenwich as well as when it docked in Bermuda. One day in the late '30s, however, he came in for a "wee bit of" a drink and sandwich and did not leave so quickly as that was the day he met my mom, Ellen. It did not take long for him to become a favorite with Mom's family in spite of the fact that he was Irish (Nick had already broken the barrier by marrying Frances Murphy) and I was told many times over that Dad was treated just like a son (no better, no worse). They married on March 25, 1940 and he became one of the team.

Uncle Porky, Mom, and Dad on Steamboat Road, circa 1939.

Within a few years after this time, many of our family, including Dad and Uncles Nick and Porky, were being drafted into the service as World War II was underway. Before he was drafted, Nick took a job at Pratt and Whitney for several months, but did not find it satisfying. Eventually, the Army called and requested his service.

Porky, on the other hand, seemed to be playing a lot of golf around the country, as well as with my dad in Bermuda where both of them had won several tournaments, singly and as partners. In the fall of 1942, a Bermuda newspaper article, describing one of Porky's wins wrote that he was "the owner of the famous 19th Hole Nightclub at Greenwich, Connecticut which is the rendezvous for Westchester Golf stars." [4] This may have been an exaggeration in more ways than one, but he obviously still had a vested interest in the business at this time. Eventually in 1943, both Porky and Dad had their golfing careers halted as they were drafted into the service, and whatever business was transacted at The 19th Hole must have been managed by the family.

Uncle Tony was older and was not drafted. His golfing career continued, although I'm sure the war and its effects had changed people's focus. It was, to say the least, challenging.

To the best of my knowledge and from reports I have read, when called into service, Nick started in the Army as a cook. However, sometime during his time in the military he was injured by a tank and was hospitalized which resulted in an early release. Years later, he used a slogan at the restaurant, "thanks for tanks," which probably had a huge double meaning for him. Porky worked at an army hospital in California and also was a cook. Dad, too, became a cook but he was sent to Germany and Austria.

While Nick and Porky (as well as many of the other males in the country) were gone, business at 557 (the address is often listed as 559 Steamboat Road as well, as the property was connected) had waned and it was questionable if it would be worthwhile to continue it. The women in the family did the best they could to keep the business going as the men went off to war. Each one of them pitched in to do her part. Little was said in my family about those difficult days regarding the business or the war until years later when Dad's army trunk was opened and we asked him a few questions. I think he and most of the soldiers just repressed those memories as well as they could and got on with their lives when they came home from the front.

Soon after the war ended, Uncle Tony and my dad opened a small golfing range that served food and was also called The 19th Hole just off the Old Post Road on Laddin's Rock Road in Stamford, Connecticut. (Apparently, this duplication of names was not a conflict back in those days, and in addition, the original 19th Hole was being reorganized around this time.) The restaurant in Stamford served light meals and beverages and it provided a living.

Around the same time, Uncle Nick put aside his law education. He decided to put his cooking, business, and showmanship skills to work. He dreamed of opening a full-scale restaurant and he urged his family to join in helping him. He also decided to capitalize on the well-known and respected name of Tony Manero for the business. (Tony's name was also originally Mainiero.) Nick changed the name of The 19th Hole in Greenwich to Manero's and he legally changed the spelling of his name to Manero as well. It was not long after that opening in 1946 that the Manero's legacy began. (This date varies from 1945 to 1948 in newspaper and family accounts.)

Meanwhile, as my grandmother was getting older, it was determined that the grocery store should be phased out. According to my cousin, George Costaregni, at this time his father and mother, Dominick and Angelina, my Aunt Agnes and Uncle Tony Manero, my mom and dad (Ellen and Art Tiernan), as well as some others still lived above the restaurant. Uncle Nick and Frances (Murphy) Manero, my grandmother and her brother and sister-in-law, the Mark Anthonys lived below.

(Uncle Porky had been traveling for golf tournaments and spent a lot of time in California.) Most of the people living in the family building had children so you can imagine what a compound it was. Although it sounds pretty crowded to us, that's how people survived back then, especially those with large immigrant families. It was all about taking care of the whole family.

My memory of living over the restaurant on Steamboat Road is vague as I was probably just four when we moved out in 1951. I always loved living there with lots of family around. That was (and still is — sometimes) my idea of heaven. We played in the vacant dirt lot next to the restaurant and there was always an older cousin around to provide entertainment. My cousin, Johnny Costaregni, lived with us until he was about six, as his mom was ill, and he could always be counted on for fun. We, and my other older cousins, would do things like collect bottle caps from the vacant yard between the restaurant and a package shop next-door. We collected hundreds of these in a variety of colors and for a young child of that time, they were treasures. Still today when I see a bottle cap or a reproduction I am carried back with happy memories to days of no cares and concerns, just pure joy.

One of my memories of living over that restaurant involved the story of Grandma and the chicken. Grandma Grace was a traditional woman of her time with a chunky frame and a round happy face. She wore dark dresses and black tied-up shoes. She would often provide the meals for all of her extended family when she had the time and the money. Long before steaks were available to her and when money was still tight, she purchased a large chicken to feed her family a special Easter meal. She had put it out on the post overnight to thaw. When she awoke the next morning and went to retrieve it, all that remained was the carcass of the chicken presided over by a well-satisfied family cat. Grandma was not happy nor was the family. A chicken was still a big meal at this time and was considered a large expense; it was back to basic soup (not shrimp bisque). Making and keeping money was still a challenge. As for the cat, he went on to live out the rest of his eight remaining lives.

It was expected in Italian families that everyone participate in making the family business a success. In the beginning, my grandmother was in charge of the kitchen help, cleaning the potatoes by the hundreds, making salads, creating soup out of nothing and cleaning up afterwards. One of her helpers was Mary Mainiero Margenot, her eldest daughter, born in Italy. Mary thought of many of her family members as another generation because she had raised many of them. Her oldest son, Albert, was born the same year as my Aunt Agnes, so Aunt Mary was out of the family home when my grandmother was still having children. My Aunt Mary, in the book (previously mentioned) written about her entitled *An Enterprising Woman, Mary Mainiero Margenot,* says that Uncle Nick would collect ration stamps (something that they would have to do to buy meat in those days) and store the meat until he finally got enough of these stamps to start the business. Here is a quote from Aunt Mary:

> And the next thing you know he started a steak house. Of course, he had no icebox then. He used to call me up on a weekend. He says: "Don't go anywhere today, Mary, because I need you this weekend." I says, "Why?" He says: "Well, I need the ice." So I would call all the tenants and get the ice out of the freezer and all the ice I could make. He had no ice maker. What we went through! I would bring the ice.

Mary relates in the book that she and her husband had a very successful business, Greenwich Iron Works. Feeling sorry for her mom working so hard, she would go into the restaurant in her silk dress, see her mom working in the kitchen, and help her clean potatoes. She relates:

> I remember washing dishes for them because there was no dishwasher. One night I happened to go down there. It was a winter night. They used to have two barrels in the kitchen. This was a steak house, the steak business was going very well. And I remember these two barrels and I saw the butcher throw the steak ends in one barrel and the fat in the other barrel. So I said to my mother in Italian:

"What do you do with this stuff here?"

"Oh," she says, "The fatta man takes it." The "fatta man, you know."

I said, "He takes two barrels?"

She says, "Yes."

So I looked where the ends of the steaks come in and I says, "Well, this is all good meat. Why does the fat man take it?"

"Aw, he takes everything," she says to me.

So I looked at the barrel at the steak. Years ago, you couldn't buy chopped meat. You had to have stamps in order to buy chopped meat, fifty cents a pound. So my brother came into the kitchen. I said, "Why do you give this stuff to the fat man?"

He said, "What am I going to do with it?"

I said, "People are hollering and crying for chopped meat. People are going crazy. Fifty, fifty-five cents a pound. Why can't you grind it up and use it for chopped meat?"

He says, "You're kidding?"

I says, "No, I'm not kidding. You take this meat." I took the piece of meat. "You take the fat off there and you chop it up. You've got chopped meat. You've got the best chopped meat in the world." He says he didn't have an automatic chopper. I says, "Buy the chopper. Buy an automatic." The next day he bought one.

The next thing he wanted to know how to sell it. "Advertise it. Put it in the paper. Fifty cents a pound." Finally he couldn't buy enough meat to chop and sell. That's what started the butcher shop. The next thing I says, "Buy a place."

He says, "Well, I ain't got the money."

I says, "Get the money."[5]

Soon Aunt Mary was asked to work for Uncle Nick but she was an entrepreneur in her own right. She did not want to work for him so she offered to be his partner. She had the money and he did not. But Uncle Nick, already on the road to success, did not want a partner, and according to Mary's oral history, she claimed that he was always a little jealous of her, as to my understanding, she was a shining star in an Italian family where women were not supposed to outshine the men.

The restaurant was soon to become solely Nick's domain. Day by day and night by night, he put his skills to work making friends with his outgoing personality, and making business decisions which would pay off handsomely.

Uncle Nick made generous use of a World War II slogan, previously mentioned: "thanks for tanks." War sentiment was still strong and Nick would run many promotional events for men and women who had served in the war effort, giving them special deals in thanks for their service to our country. This added to the great affection and admiration that many were beginning to develop for the Manero name.

So life moved on and the business was becoming successful. Family members worked in the business to insure a dependable work force and some security. In addition to Grandma and Mary helping out, my Aunt Lina used to care for Nick's big chef hats, washing, starching, and ironing them to keep them fresh. My mom and Aunt Agnes would also help when needed in the kitchen. Inevitably as in any large family, squabbles ensued and jealousy raised its ugly head.

As time went on and things got better for all in the late '40s and early '50s, the family moved out, one by one, to pursue their own versions of the American dream. Uncle Dominick and his wife, Aunt Lina Costaregni, who spent a considerable amount of time in and out of hospitals with epilepsy, bought property right down the street on Davenport Avenue and moved there with their three sons, George, Danny, and John (Nick later bought this property for $25,000 to expand the parking lot for the meat market). Aunt Agnes and Uncle Tony, who by this time had their two sons, Dick and Bob, bought a lovely home in a beautiful section of Greenwich on Lita Drive. My mom and dad, Ellen and Art Tiernan, bought a sweetheart of a home on Havemeyer Lane in Old Greenwich (where my younger brother Peter and I lived only a couple of years before we moved to Florida). Uncle Nick and Aunt Fran bought a sprawling place on Glenville Road which they called "the farm" and lived there with my cousins Lita and Nick Jr. The property has remained in Nick's family for about seven decades.

By the time my grandmother died in the early '50s, Nick had well established himself as the head of the business and the de facto leader. These were the days when the oldest Italian son inherited the business, but in fairness to Uncle Nick, he is the one who brought it to the success that it was, certainly with much family help.

Unfortunately, this leadership did not occur without more than a little in-family fighting, as Uncle Porky, the second son, was also interested in restaurateuring. Porky had lots of business experience by that time and he was an extremely sociable person though he never had the drive or working spirit Nick had. Not only was he a pro golfer but by this time he had spent years in California as an "agent." He knew many famous people and that was good for networking. However, dependability was not his forte and that reputation within the family did not serve him well. He would be just as happy on the golf course or at a racetrack or buzzing round in his convertible as he was at a fancy (for those days) restaurant. I loved Uncle Porky. He was just plain fun. In later years, however, I came to recognize how many of his own family called him "a playboy" or a "ladies man." Many family photographs show him as the dapper Italian hunk of the times. In spite of that, in the mid-'50s, Uncle Porky settled down in Connecticut and started his own restaurants, most probably with Uncle Nick's help.

The transition at Grandma's death was not that easy, and in fact, was more of a battle. I distinctly remember my mom, the peacemaker, writing letters back and forth to her two brothers urging them to get along with one another. She must have had a lot of intestinal fortitude putting herself in the middle of this family squabble. She was like a referee in a boxing ring. Rumors of fights among the two were legendary.

After Grandma Grace died, Uncle Nick offered to buy out the remaining estate left to each of the family members. Some felt pushed out and others were delighted to have the cash. He paid $7000 per member, and for some reason that I never understood until reading the book on Aunt Mary, she, the oldest sister, got $10,000.[6] By this time my mom and dad had an agreement to go to Florida to establish a southern

Manero's. Soon after, Uncle Porky had opened his own place in Orange, Connecticut, and was quite successful. Eventually, he also opened his restaurant in Westport, which was relocated after the state bought his property. According to some newspaper reports, he may also have had some ownership with Nick in some restaurants in the beginning.

Uncle Tony, who by this time had his own successful restaurant on Old Post Road, was asked by Nick to come back to eliminate the competition. After a while he agreed and worked there as host for many years until his retirement.

The Experience

Although we so often talk about an overnight success, in reality, there are very few overnight successes. Nick and the entire Manero family, together with their mother, should be credited for the success that Manero's came to be. There was no question that Nick, the oldest son, was in charge but credit should be given also to brothers and sisters, brothers-in-law, sisters-in-law, nieces, nephews, and cousins, all of whom helped the original grocery, bar and grill, restaurant and/or nightclub businesses survive the war years, as well as the late '40s and the early '50s. In addition, the name, magnetism, and success of Tony Manero in the golf world cannot be underestimated. I have always felt that Uncle Tony was not given the credit he deserved in helping to make the business a huge success. Through many family squabbles, disagreements, jealousies, reunions, weddings, illnesses, funerals, and other family challenges, the Manero family restaurant, known as Manero's Steak House, survived, and thrived.

Warner LeRoy tells us that: "A restaurant is a fantasy — a kind of living fantasy in which diners are the most important members of the cast." Much more than a meal, eating at Manero's was a fantasy experience. There was magic happening in the air across from the docks. To set the scene on Steamboat Road, long before you ever parked your 1955 Pontiac on the lot, you would smell the garlic. It would fill your nostrils and permeate every piece of clothing you were wearing. Upon exiting your car, the scent of medium rare steaks sparked your senses and by the time you entered the front door of the restaurant, you were begging to be seated. You'd be cordially greeted by Uncle Tony, the host. Then, Uncle Nick, a large, jolly, and handsome man, as often as possible (and when he was not putting out literal or figurative fires in the kitchen or elsewhere) would seat you with much fanfare and chatter. Many times he would usher you through the kitchen where you could view the organized chaos in an attempt to get to a table without everyone knowing you were cutting through the line. He did this so often over the years that people got wise to his ways.

By the time you were seated, you would be ravenous. The feast would begin. The waiters, mostly golfers of old country Italian, Irish, or Polish backgrounds, would make you feel at home with their boisterous small talk and their attention. They made sure your water glasses were filled as you reviewed the menu, shaped as a black and white chef's hat, and by today's standards, very simple. A cocktail would be next if desired but it was not really about the dividend drinks that Manero's has always provided. It was about the beef. No fancy sauces or accompaniments. Your meal, most likely, would start with garlic bread, the incredible Gorgonzola cheese salad, maybe a shrimp cocktail (about as haute cuisine as it got) and then the piece de résistance: the steak with onion rings and a huge potato dripping with butter. I'm sure there were vegetables but no one seems to remember. If they were on the plate they paled in comparison to the rest. No one worried about diet or health while eating at Manero's.

Back then, even in upscale Greenwich, Connecticut, it was perfectly fine to go to dinner and have the garlic bread and butter oozing down your face to your chin and onto your clothes. In addition, the Gorgonzola salad was loaded with cheese and Manero's special Gorgonzola dressing. It was common to see people in all strata of society take the Italian bread and mop up every remaining drop of oil and vinegar and little cheese chunks that remained in their bowls. Those were the days of the old wooden bowls, now forbidden by health departments. Another favorite was the bowl of onion rings, breaded and fried to a golden brown to top off one's meal. Add all these (about three thousand calories so far) to the succulent T-bone steaks, done medium rare and a great big baked potato. Could anything be better? (I'm drooling and thinking of running over to our Manero's right now.) Those were the days before widespread cholesterol or fat consciousness and even cardiologists would stand in line to indulge.

It was this type of fare that would attract customers from all over the Northeast. People would come from New York City, Long Island, Westchester County, Yonkers, the Bronx, nearby regions of New Jersey and all of Connecticut to have a meal like this. Uncle Nick captured the market there long before anyone else set foot in the area. Nick had a variety of ways of making people feel special — especially children and women. In addition to the well-known birthday song (see Happy Birthday section), he would visit each table and chat on a variety of current topics. He complimented women in writing on the many wooden signs on the wall displaying lines like "beautiful women eat steak to stay that way." He would give out a variety of souvenirs to the children and always a lollipop before they left. I remember those old lollipops with the floppy U-shaped sticks. They were called "safety pops" and were so good. Match covers, promotions, and menus were given to the adults. Everyone went away happy.

Golfers were a favorite group to visit Manero's Steak House. Nearby there were several of the most desirable courses in the country such as Westchester and Winged Foot. It was not uncommon on any given night to have Sam Sneed, Arnold Palmer, or in later years, Jack Nicklaus show up for a huge meal. Since Tony Manero, Nick's brother-in-law, won the 1936 National Open and was the host of the restaurant, many thought that he owned the restaurant and they flocked in to see him. After Tony greeted them and sometimes seated them, Nick would take over the show.

From the 1960s, Manero's was well known in the area. I remember watching Johnny Carson late one night in the mid-'60s and jolting up out of my bed to hear Johnny talking about the incredible food at Manero's. Andy Rooney was a frequent guest as well and wrote many stories about the restaurant. Nick hosted Loretta Young, Buster Crabbe, Bert Parks, Johnny Olsen, and a variety of other entertainers of the time. Celebrities, golfers, and businessmen would bring their buddies, constituents, girlfriends, and families to enjoy the great food and the ambience provided by Nick and the T-Boners, the name given to the waiters who accompanied him in song. The happy birthday song became famous and was recorded. After each song, all the guests in the restaurant would chime in and applaud. It was magical.

Uncle Nick in front of Manero's on Steamboat Road.

Nick Manero had, as Oscar Wilde would say, "a form of genius." His concept was a forerunner of many a restaurant concept and Uncle Nick, the brilliant business and creative promotional person, went all out to make sure people were happy. The product was delicious and people had no problem gorging themselves. The service and Manero's hospitality was personalized. Throw in a little homespun entertainment and it was a great memory maker. A steak dinner was the opium of the middle and upper-middle classes and what everyone wanted when they went out to eat.

Bill Masucci, a customer of Manero's in Greenwich and now of Palm City, currently living in the Vero Beach area shared with me a story about a bachelor party held at Manero's the night before an elegant Greenwich wedding. He wrote:

> Went to dinner at Manero's. Had lots of the world-famous Gorgonzola cheese salad. Ordered many loaves of garlic bread. Interesting to see grown men fighting for the last piece of garlic bread to wipe the inside of the wooden salad bowl. Nick, with his high chef's hat, wished the groom good luck. At the wedding the next day, the ushers, including me, were standing in the reception line. We were only shaking hands as no one wanted to kiss us. The bride was upset. They were grossed out. We ate many Sen-Sens, the original breath freshener. Still…the breath freshener, gulped down by the handfuls, did not work.

Bill wasn't kidding about the Gorgonzola cheese and garlic bread. I have heard of many professionals who canceled their afternoon appointments after "lunching" at any of the Manero's.

Always Bring the Children

Our Manero's motto since the start has been "always bring the children," which according to family history was established by Aunt Agnes, Tony's wife. She was a beautiful woman in all ways and having no daughters, she was like a second mother to me. Because she was the wife of a star in the golf world, she spent a lot of time in a supportive role, and had a lot of long days waiting for her golfer-husband to play his rounds, especially in the early years before she had kids. She was crazy about kids so "always bring the children" would have been her style. It has been our motto for seventy years, long before it was fashionable to have children at more upscale restaurants. Those were the days when family structure was quite different and discipline was much stricter. Kids did not act up at meals. If they did they were taken outside.

We love children and love to see them dine with their families. "Always bring the children" has served us well but amidst all the dining controversy with today's children, I often wonder if these days, Aunt Agnes would put a qualifier in her motto. Most of the families who dine with us are respectful of how their kids behave at meals, but every once in a while we get a touchy situation. Today, if we upset a customer in any way it will soon be on Trip Advisor, Yellow Pages, Google, Yelp, Twitter, or any other of the social media before the kids are even strapped back into their car seats.

Happy Birthday

Memory is a powerful bridge across time. If I had only a quarter for every time I heard the story about Nick and the T-Boners singing "Happy Birthday," I would be wealthier than the Oracle of Omaha. The Manero's birthday song was almost as good a memory maker as the scent of the garlic bread.

No matter in which part of the restaurant I am standing in our Manero's in Palm City, I personally hear stories or hear echoes of someone telling Jay, Joyce, Danielle, Pam, or anyone of our team the stories of how, when they were young, their parents would take them to Manero's for their birthday and how Nick and the waiters would sing "Happy Birthday" to them, and then present them with ice cream cake. Nick would be dressed in his white apron, a long sleeve striped shirt, neatly laundered and starched, and donned in one of his signature hats he had designed by Lily Dache, a New York designer of the times. His waiters were all dressed in their red aprons with Maneros' chef hat logo. He would pull out his tuning instrument — a pitch pipe, slowly look around at all his "boys" as the restaurant would come to a quick and deafening silence. They would test-sing the note projected from the instrument and then the song began. For effect, he'd often start over again if it was not to his liking. They sung a capella, in rich baritone voices. It was an indescribable show of monumental proportions. You really had to be there to appreciate it.

All service stopped while this happened and it would happen several times a night — but none of the other customers seemed to mind. In fact, it was part of the entertainment you expected at Manero's.

Although other restaurants have tried to replicate this, none have come close. Uncle Nick commanded the dining room and the song.

The happy birthday song was sung in spurts like this:

> Happy birthday...*three second pause*...to you,
> Happy birthday...*three second pause*...to you,
> Happy birth...*pause*...day…*pause*...to Susie (*hitting a high note on the last syllable and holding it*),
> Happy birth...*pause*...day…*pause*...to you (*sung with a snap*)!

After each song the restaurant would erupt with wild applause. Incredibly, as simple as it sounds today, the memory of the event has been living in the hearts and minds of thousands of people from ages thirty-five to one hundred. I have heard stories that it was even sung on the Ed Sullivan Show in New York City. The song was recorded and can still be found occasionally in its original 45 recording on eBay and similar places. I have a copy of this recording and playing it always makes me smile.

Uncle Nick was a showman and educated businessman who had all the confidence of the eldest son in the Italian family. Even though he had a law background, he preferred to create his life and his livelihood around food, hospitality, and the golfing world. He was an incredible catalyst for the success that would come to all Manero's Steak Houses and Restaurants in future years. Few restaurateurs have made such a mark on the memories of so many in at least three generations of people from a wide background in the Northeast. There are some great pictures of him with his team that can be found on the internet that give a flavor of his expertise.

The Butcher Shop

Complementing the popularity of the restaurant, one of the most successful parts of the business was Manero's butcher shop and retail market. People would come from miles to purchase their supplies of

Manero's beef, which was aged up to twenty-eight days right there on the premises. I have read reports that have been grossly exaggerated saying the shop brought in millions of dollars each week. Remember, I am writing about the '60s and '70s and beef was much cheaper, so do the math. That said, it was hugely successful with the well-to-do in the Greenwich area. Amidst many reports of pilferage and deal making by some employees in the early years, the butcher shop raked in gigantic profits. When my cousin, Nick, closed the business in 2006, one of the employees who worked there opened up his own shop in Greenwich on the very property once owned by my Grandmother Grace's sister and brother-in-law, the Schintos. There on Bruce Park Avenue they had operated their own small grocery store decades earlier. Life certainly can be circuitous.

We're Going to Manero's

I remember the frigid wintry night when I took a group of my college roommates to Manero's in Greenwich in January of 1966. It was my first year at Manhattanville College in nearby Purchase, New York, and I was far from home — about 1300 miles or so from the little town of Hallandale, Florida. Although Hallandale was small at the time, my high school, South Broward in Hollywood, was not. We had a huge class of about eight hundred girls and boys and there was always a lot of fun and excitement. I had chosen Manhattanville, a small Catholic girls school at the time, for many reasons, not the least of which was that it was fifteen minutes from my extended family in Greenwich and one of my cousins, Dick Manero, whose opinion I respected, encouraged me to go there. In addition, I would be close to my favorites: Aunt Agnes, Dick and Bob's mom in Greenwich, and my Aunt Eileen in Harrison, New York. It was a great choice and in addition to wonderful weekends with my favorite aunts, and cousins, I received a superb education in my chosen field of psychology. I had already determined that I would become a psychologist as I was fascinated by studying people's behavior.

While Manhattanville was known for many good things, the cafeteria food was not one of them, so taking the gals to Manero's was a real treat. My friends were all so excited — these young women from all over the country, Dee from Utica, Penny from suburban Boston, Toni from Mamaroneck, a gal from the Seychelle Islands, and several others. They had already heard so much from friends and people around campus about Manero's in Greenwich. Toni had been there many times as she lived close by and recanted many happy stories of her visits to the restaurant. In any event, many of my college friends had heard mouth-watering stories from her and others.

These gals were all from well-to-do homes. Their fathers were businessmen, doctors, lawyers, investment bankers and the like. They ended up at Manhattanville College of the Sacred Heart with the Madams who had taught generations of well-to-do families, including the Kennedys. How I ended up there, I am not quite sure. At Manhattanville, we would get great educations, great social training, and maybe even catch a husband, as it was the era in which women were just transitioning from stay-at-home hostesses to the workplace. Most of my roommates did choose the workplace and many, after graduation, went on to great careers or vocations.

So the trip to Manero's was long-awaited. Actually, anything to get us off campus was a delight as the campus was small by today's standards and located in an exclusive, secluded enclave of Purchase, New York, right down the street from the home of Robert Goulet. Not a lot of activity happened there during long winter days, and other than a couple of pubs not far from campus there were not many places to go. At the time, New York State's drinking age was eighteen so on the weekends these places were goldmines, overwhelmed with students from Manhattanville and eventually from SUNY at Purchase. But partying was limited by today's standards as these were the ancient days of check-ins and check-outs, curfews, and limited weekends away. Oh, how the world has changed.

But...back to Manero's. Upon arriving at Manero's, my Uncles Tony and Nick greeted us all and treated us in style. The young women were complimented, fussed over, and offered anything they wished to eat. We ate lavish meals, not missing any of the specialties for which Manero's was known and we relished every morsel.

The décor of Manero's was what my cousin, Dick Manero, appropriately described as "fashionably shabby." It had wooden walls with mostly golfing pictures, in simple brown wood frames all around. It had plain, noisy, wooden floors, simple tables (many of which were constructed by my father years ago) with paper placemats featuring the Manero's logo. The tables were crowded together with straight-backed Polish chairs with black and red vinyl seat covers. By this time the place had grown from its original fifty seats, but was not yet at the 600 mark where it eventually ended up.

Times were different, but no one, even then, would call it anything but unattractive, at best. People came to Manero's for the experience. It did not matter at all what the place looked like because the Greenwich crowds came not for the décor but for the food and the show. In those days, I'm sure Uncle Nick, the showman par excellence, got away with a lot which would not be tolerated or considered politically correct today, but then, so did everyone else. People left their experience at Manero's charmed, entertained, stuffed, happy, and anticipating their next visit. And so did the fine young ladies from Manhattanville.

> *One does not discover new lands without
> consenting to lose sight of the shore for a very long time.*
> —Andre Gide

CHAPTER TWO

Manero's in Hallandale, Florida

My Dad

My dad's family was small in comparison to Mom's family but was filled with step-aunts and uncles and cousins whom, for the most part, I never knew. Rumor had it that his father, Bernard Tiernan (I never knew him), had five wives, outliving each one of them before marrying the next. My dad always got upset when my mom related that questionable piece of information. To be sure, we know that he had three wives. His middle wife was my grandma, Frances Whalen. She collapsed and died in their kitchen in front of my dad and his younger sister, also Frances, when Dad was four years old. From that point on, Dad was brought up by his father and his favorite, Aunt Margaret, and then later, his stepmother, Emily, for whom he had much affection. Unfortunately, his sister, Frances, and he were separated as she went to live with another family member. In spite of that, Dad and Frances remained very close throughout their lives. The gift of that relationship for me is her daughter, Susan Fruzen, my cousin, with whom I am very close.

When Dad was a young boy, he traveled alongside his father wherever he went. Grandpa Tiernan was a successful builder in the early and mid-'20s in South Florida, especially in Miami and Coral Gables. (Dad must have learned the crafting and building skills to make the original tables at Manero's in Greenwich from him.) When times were good, Grandpa and my dad played a lot of golf together but when the 1926 hurricane hit it helped usher in the Great Depression in South Florida and my grandfather lost everything. The 1929 Crash further devastated that economy cutting off the expensive world of golf to my dad who was sixteen and quite promising at the sport. The excitement and challenge of golf was closed to him for a while, at least in the way he knew it. So Dad, in love with the game of golf and not easily dissuaded, began to caddy.

Dad, the young golfer.

Later in his late teens and early twenties, Dad worked on cruise ships that would come back and forth between Greenwich Harbor and Bermuda. When he reached either side, the first thing he would do was get up a foursome for a game of golf. Well known as a gifted golfer, he had become a pro and was sought out by Nick, Porky, and even Tony for a game when he was in town. He won several tournaments and was on track for greater ones when a lovely woman walked into his life. It was during one of those trips back and forth from Bermuda in the late thirties that he met my mom at The 19th Hole in Greenwich. He started coming back often when he was in town, sometimes once or more a day. After a while, it was a frequent occurrence as he had fallen in love with my mom, Ellen Mainiero.

The Letter

By the early 1940s the war had already started in Europe and life seemed to be changing quickly. Dad was twenty-seven at the time and was in Miami in early March when he wrote this note home to his Aunt Margaret, who had helped raise him. It seemed to be a rushed note as Dad sounded pretty desperate to get the baptismal certificate in order to get married. It wasn't his usual and gracious style; he seemed to have gotten right to the point. I have dozens of letters that he later wrote in the early '40s to my Aunt Margaret and his cousin, Marie, who saved them all. After she passed away, I found them neatly categorized in a shoebox. What a gift as they told me so much about his life and experiences in the war.

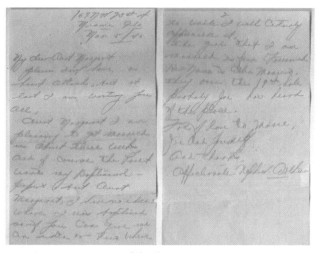

The letter.

Mom and Dad were married in Miami on March 25, 1940, the day after Easter in Gesu Church in Miami, as those were the times when you couldn't get married in the Catholic Church during Easter. Uncle Porky was his best man. Mom and Dad traveled back to Greenwich and Dad resumed his golfing career and soon won the Bermuda Open in 1942. Next to Mom, golf was his life at that time and our family has numerous newspaper articles of the golfing tournaments played by Dad, Uncle Tony, and Uncle Porky. But soon golf was to be interrupted as he was drafted in the spring of 1943 and the following year, sent to war. He was a cook in the U.S. Army and by the time he returned home he was able to do just about any job in the kitchen. He was in the European Theater of Operations in the 71st Infantry Division. His skills were admired by his commanding officer General Willard G. Wyman, who told Dad that he was the only one in the Army who cold cook rare roast beef the way he liked it. Dad spent sixty-two days in combat before the war ended. He remained in Bavaria for about six to eight months after the war ended during which time he and General Wyman played a lot of golf together. When he returned to the States, he opened a business in Stamford, Connecticut with Uncle Tony, which was also called The 19th Hole, and he helped Uncle Nick on the side. This business was later sold when Manero's in Greenwich became busier. Nick had asked him to come to work for him full time and he agreed.

My mom was an extraordinarily good woman. She would do anything for anyone. She was creative with her hands, was a trained seamstress, and of course, helped out at Manero's in Greenwich when needed. Had she been better educated, she may have become a writer. Over the years, she composed great letters to everyone and in her later years wrote a small column for our local paper, the *Hallandale Digest*. She was even named "Woman of the Year" by our local Chamber of Commerce. She had keen abilities as a businesswoman as well and knew how to save a dollar. She was a fighter and would never let anyone get the best of her. Mom was determined that the daughter in her family would get as much education as the son (thank you, Mom) as she didn't want her own family history repeated. Though she was the disciplinarian in our family she was never difficult or harsh as her father had been. She was challenged by bipolar disease, which was exacerbated by the memories of a violent father. She had high energy, a sometimes benefit of bipolar disease, believed in lots of community involvement and although she had a couple of tough spells with her illness, thanks to the love of my dad, she had a good and productive life. She was consumed by the Catholic faith, which back in those days was filled with fearful exhortations.

My dad was smart, had high emotional intelligence and a well-integrated work ethic. He was loved by people both off and on the golf course for his gentle and light-hearted Irish ways, fostered by his aunt and later his stepmom. I could never understand why he didn't have anger issues over losing his mother at such a young age, but he had none. Apparently the love of his dad along with the caring women in his life made up for his great loss. He and my mom were a great team and became well known in the Hallandale area and soon the restaurant, like the restaurant in Greenwich, was to become successful. However, this did not happen overnight and not without eight hard years of challenging work.

Dad during his army days with my cousin, John Costaregni.

Our Trip to Hallandale

My cousin, John Costaregni, recently reminded me of the first trip we made to Florida in 1952. It was an investigational trip to find a location for a Manero's South. Mom, Dad, brother Peter, cousin John, and I left from Greenwich, Connecticut, and traveled in our Buick along Routes 301, 17, and 441 (not much of 1-95 was open back then except maybe around New Jersey) for three delightful (the kids thought) days. These were the days of long unevenly paved roads and inner-city excursions around Baltimore, Washington, Richmond, and Jacksonville. I remember wanting to live in those cities where there were always groups of children and adults chattering on porches. Looking back, I'm sure they were living in poverty but the aspect of community life always appealed to me. We stopped in the rural communities of Virginia and Georgia for dinners and overnight stays. Cotton was sprinkled all over the roads in the Carolinas and Georgia and tobacco was growing in prolific amounts on both sides of the highway.

I still recall the incredible southern fried chicken and grits in one South Carolina restaurant on Route 301. In Georgia, we loaded up on peaches and pecans to enjoy on the trip. My dad made this trip many times over the years with his father, and once we moved to Florida, we made it at least once a year for many more years. Dad came to know the route like the back of his hand and could tell you where to stop for anything you needed in any of these small towns, remote and sparse by our standards. Dad always used to leave apples in the car overnight on these trips, and still today the smell of apples stirs my emotions.

After three days of traveling, we arrived in Florida where we encountered lots of sunshine. Palmetto bugs were everywhere and acres of mangrove swamps surrounded us. There were millions of what we came to know as land crabs. As a six-year-old child, I found these ugly monsters terrifying, like something from a horror movie.

Among the locations we scouted was the building on 1900 East Beach Boulevard (later the address was changed to 2600) with a restaurant on the first floor and apartments upstairs. Mom and Dad thought this might work well. We were used to this arrangement and it would make it easy to be together as a family unit with long hard restaurant nights. We looked at several other restaurants, one being the Old Heidelberg, which was next to the dog track on U.S. 1 in Hallandale. Finally, Mom and Dad made their choice. It was the location on the Intracoastal Waterway, next to a decrepit drawbridge on a two-lane highway. There was nothing on the west side of the drawbridge but the building. I mean *nothing*.

My parents were excited and reported their findings to Nick. Within a few days the purchase date was determined. The building was bought by my parents, Uncle Nick Manero, and Dan Dowd, who was also in business at a Manero's in Paramus, New Jersey. Dan and his brother had been trusted employees. They were butchers who had worked for Uncle Nick and had done very well; well enough to invest with us in Florida. From what my parents told me, each put in eight thousand dollars. In a few short years, my parents and uncle bought out Dan Dowd. Uncle Nick, Mom, and Dad continued as partners for many years until 1986 when my parents retired.

They purchased the property in the days when the entertaining Arthur Godfrey broadcast daily shows from Miami Beach. We were not far from the action. However, the only thing famous about Hallandale in those years was that the American divorcee, Mrs. Wallace Simpson and the never to be King Edward VIII, reportedly stayed close by for an extended vacation in a well-known old hotel (I believe it was called the Hampshire House). In addition, the famous Gulfstream Race Track was about a mile down the street. This provided a lot of activity with an influx of people during the racing season each year.

Early Hallandale Years

The building, which housed the new restaurant, was built around 1950. Together with the bar it seated about two hundred. Later when things got better, my parents did a series of remodels and were able to double the occupancy. On the second floor there were three two-unit apartments and two studios with a large patio comprised of a white stone pebble floor.

We settled into the first two apartments. When things got better, we took a third apartment and a whole renovation was done. Eventually we took over the whole upstairs. Still…I wanted to live in a new three-bedroom, two-bath home, which at the time cost about eight to ten thousand dollars. Even though Mom and Dad looked at homes, they felt we should live over the restaurant in order to be close to the business. I believe they loved and reverted to the old European idea of living over the shop, an idea which is becoming popular again today in upscale business communities. Looking back, this setup provided for one of the most interesting, educational, diverse, and wonderful childhoods I could ever have imagined.

Manero's in Hallandale, circa, 1953

Soon after we arrived and settled into our living quarters, my parents moved the liquor store from the east to the west side of the building, next to the bar. Behind the bar was either Frankie or Marty or Mike or my dad. Whoever it was, he was friendly, chatty, and one semester short of a psychology degree. The bar had all kinds of characters and was full each day. These were the days of the two martini lunches that oftentimes flowed into dinner. On many an afternoon an employee would take a customer's keys and drive him or her home followed by another staff member who would return the driver to the restaurant. The bar was large, a four-sided wraparound with an entrance for the bartender and supplies on the kitchen side. There were about ten booths of various sizes. Within a short time the bar was a sought-out place to dine.

Beyond the bar there was a large kitchen, big enough to accommodate business for a couple of decades. In the corner of the bar was a large walk-in cooler with a window, so the steaks and beef could be displayed. Next to that was a case which held a few of the famous Manero's chef hats. Underneath this corner case was the jukebox, my favorite piece of equipment. It was constantly belting out songs by Peggy Lee, Frank Sinatra, Dean Martin, Patti Page, Bing Crosby, and other favorites of the day. To the left of the bar and next to the cooler was the entrance to the dining room. You had to go through the bar to get to the dining room, but later a more elegant entrance was opened on the waterfront bordering the Intracoastal Waterway.

In the beginning, things were difficult. A few people from Greenwich joined us to help us get started. After all, who would not want to work in Florida back then? I remember most of them staying for only a season because it was not the instant success that they expected. The first season was good but short and then there were the next eight months to endure before it started again. Mom and Dad worked together with their small but dedicated staff. I am sure my mom said many rosaries each night, as things were not exactly as expected in those first years.

A South Florida land crab. Picture courtesy of Steven Jaconski.

Land Crabs

Within a few days of our move to Hallandale in the late summer of 1953, my brother Peter and I became both fascinated and horrified by the silly looking creatures with oval-shaped crustacean bodies, about six to eight inches wide with eight legs, one huge claw and one small claw to balance. They were usually gray, blue, or beige in color. They had two ugly "googly" eyes that stood up like flags on their frame; they crawled all over the streets and sidewalks of Hallandale in the early fall.

Land crabs were prolific in Florida. But the worst thing about them was that they covered the roadways making it impossible to travel from A1A to U.S. 1, without crunching thirty to fifty of them at a time. The stench (I will never forget it) was overwhelming, enough to make you nauseous. Many a tire was destroyed by these creatures. I was told that they were more afraid of us than we were of them but that was a small consolation.

The first year they terrified us. By the second year, we began to get used to seeing them, but never to that terrible smell. We also realized that many of the locals had lots of fun with these creatures with their yearly land crab races, which attracted many of the young kids in the area. By the third year, it had become our job to shoo them away so that the customers could get through the doors. We would use a broom but sometimes they would escape our reach and get in through the doors. Then we'd have to get my dad (or another grownup) to come and get them out as people would not respond well to dining in restaurants with land crabs.

They inhabited our town in droves until about the early '60s when their presence became rare. By the late '60s, they almost became extinct in our area, due to the construction. Fifteen years ago I was walking down the waterfront in Stuart, Florida, and lo and behold, I found one walking along the water's edge. The years had not been kind to them as they only look uglier, albeit a whole lot less scary than they were in my Hallandale days.

Cash Debit

When things get rough, I think of how difficult my parents really had it in those early years in Hallandale. It was the fall of 1953 and the restaurant was into its fifth week of operation. We all knew then as now that everyone wants to try a new restaurant in its first weeks and we were swamped with business. Mom and Dad were optimistic. The servers and bartenders could not believe their good luck at being hired by this instant success. Everyone was upbeat and even I, at age six, had a job at twenty-five cents an hour wiping the silverware that came out of the dishwasher. Life could not be better.

Unfortunately, after about a month, things began to calm down. Other restaurateurs in the area were happy again because the new place had been tried and people went back to their old favorites, perhaps integrating the new restaurant into their schedule of eating out. From our perspective it was early fall and known to be a quiet time in Florida and so Mom and Dad were not particularly concerned.

It was into the fifth week of business when the land crabs were busily scurrying away to their hiding places. It was still hot as blazes in South Florida when Dad opened the doors with his small staff and waited and waited. For the first two hours, not one person came through the doors; he began to wonder what he was doing wrong. Were the lights on? Was the road closed? Were there too many land crabs for the cars to drive down the street? What was the problem?

Finally about 7:15 p.m., a party of three came through the door and the small staff was elated. The three customers ordered drinks and then a second round — hope! Then another party of five came through the door. For the time being, our population was eight. Dad was delighted as he would be approaching one hundred dollars or more for the night — all was not lost.

The two parties seemed to be enjoying their meals as they sat together in the almost-empty dining room. Then the time came for the people to pay. Each of the parties paid with Diners Club. The first put the tip of eight dollars on his ticket and the second one put a ten-dollar tip on his Diners Club. We were out eighteen dollars in cash for the night. In those days, the Diners Club paid restaurants by mail about a week later. Dad took the cash from the cigar box, which served as our cash register for the first several months. No one else came in for the rest of the evening. The night was over and Dad was short eighteen dollars plus food costs and employee costs.

Nowadays whenever we have a bummer of a night in one of our places, and every restaurant does have them, I think of the story of the eighteen dollars, smile, look skyward, and say to myself: "Praise the Lord!"

Cousin Danny

Every family needs a rebel. And my beloved Danny was ours. At least twice a year for the first few years we were in Florida, we'd hear the report that Uncle Nick had fired my Cousin Danny Costaregni, the son of my mom's older sister Angelina (and brother to Johnny and George). Danny was a handsome devil of an Italian man in his mid-twenties. He had a thick head of beautiful dark hair and I always remember him running his hand through it. There was a rumor that he had been in the seminary for a while but I could never have imagined that. While doing my research, I was shocked to find out that not only was he in the seminary but that "Brother Costaregni" was in formation to become a Jesuit at Los Gatos, California for several years. He was written about in a book by Robert Blair Kaiser (also a Jesuit in training for several years) called *Clerical Errors*.[7] According to Kaiser, who also wrote the bestseller, *RFK Must Die!*,[8] Cousin Danny was playing football for Loyola in L.A. when he was "transfixed by the Jesuits" and felt a calling to the religious life. Also, according to Kaiser, Danny's (and my) Uncle Porky, a Hollywood agent, had made things nice for his nephew by allowing him to use his new Buick convertible to drive along Wilshire Boulevard with beautiful women sitting next to him. Apparently this did not sit well with his Jesuit formation team and it was determined (mutually?) that Danny was not cut out for the Jesuits or a life of celibacy.

It was about then that Danny's bohemian lifestyle began. After returning from California, he would work for Uncle Nick for a while, insult a customer or have some sort of a spontaneous flare-up and Nick would fire him and he would come down to Florida to my soft-hearted father who would hire him. Within a few weeks, he would be in trouble for some minor infraction like speeding or starting a fight or who knows what else. But Danny was so darn handsome, charming, and lovable. And life with Danny around was exhilarating, at least for me. You just could not stay mad at him. But he could be explosive. Dad would bail him out and he'd go back north to start this pattern all over again. This happened several times until Uncle Nick, known for congeniality, told him never to return. So…for a final time he showed up in Hallandale to continue the cycle but Mom and Dad could just not afford emotionally or financially to bail him out again. Finally, Danny went back to Connecticut and met and married a beautiful woman, Rose, and had a family.

Years later, Danny took his restaurant skills and opened Pastrami Dan's, first in Cos Cob and then on Mason Street in Greenwich, Connecticut, where it operated successfully for many years. Danny has passed now but his son and daughter-in-law, Dan and Beth, still own a successful Pastrami Dan's on the Tamiami Trail in Naples on the Gulf Coast of Florida. I have been there and can tell you that they have followed the Manero family's tradition of great food.

Thoughts of Danny always make me smile.

The Four Hammers

Mom was a woman of great persistence when she wanted to get something done. I'm sure she had acquired this intestinal fortitude as a result of a challenging childhood. She never gave up and had her own unique way of solving every problem.

Long before the use of the cell phone, my mom invented a unique and totally practical way (not sure *Shark Tank* would jump on it) of getting in touch with Dad when he did not answer the phone. Generally, Dad would go to work early in the morning, often after taking Peter and me to swim in the Atlantic Ocean before school. He would come home, shower, and then go down to work while Mom would encourage us to move along and get dressed so she could take us to school. Many days we'd still be home eating breakfast or getting ready while Dad was already working.

Dad never answered the phone at the restaurant any time before 9:30 a.m. and on weekends before noon. So Mom, wanting to speak to him but not wanting to expend the energy of going down the stairs, decided to take matters into her own hands, literally. She invested in several hammers.

Between 7:00 and 7:30 a.m., Dad would be at the register or the bar, digging out the receipts of the night before and counting the money. These were the days when a restaurant actually *had* money before heavy credit card use. If I recall correctly, the Diners Club was the most frequently used and the American Express next. Carte Blanche was another popular card though not used as much. All three accounted for about five to seven percent of the business. Today, it would be the exact opposite with cash accounting for five to ten percent of sales.

On any given morning, Mom would proceed to one of these areas of the apartment located over the exact spot where she expected Dad to be and she would bang three or four times with one of her hammers. God help him if he were not at the right place at the right time and did not immediately call. If this were to happen she would move over on top of one of the next two spots, the office or the men's room and she would begin the same process. With no response, Mom's ire would increase as her patience was being tested. If she was not successful in getting Dad's attention she would go to hammer number four over the kitchen and begin her banging. If hammer number four produced no response on the phone, she would start over again really getting her Italian up and repeating the whole process. If by chance there was no response after the second round, she would send Peter or me down with the keys and a message to "tell your Father he is in trouble!" If my father saw one of us enter the restaurant between seven and eight a.m., he knew that his goose was cooked and he could pretty well forget his afternoon golf game with the boys. Dad, a gentle and kind Irishman, jumped for the rest of his life at the sound of a hammer. Kind of like Pavlov's dog.

Dad was crazy about Mom until the day she died. She was the light of his life. I do not ever remember him complaining about this or any other of her remarkable idiosyncrasies. I have always been fond of the phrase: "Your father is the glitter but your mother is the glue." That's the way it was.

The Night of the Fire

I have heard the words "fire and restaurant" together in many of the stories my dad used to tell. Convenient fires allowed a failing business to collect insurance money. One in particular he loved to tell was about a Meyer and Nino. So Nino says, "Meyer, how did you make out after the terrible fire you had in your restaurant?" Meyer says, "Shush, Nino, it hasn't happened yet — it's scheduled for tonight."

Stories of restaurants and fires are legendary but over the years that my family has had restaurants (most of my life) we have had at least three legitimate fires in three different restaurants. The scariest was in Hallandale about 1955. The second and worst was in West Palm Beach in the mid-'70s and the last one was in the laundry room of our Maggie Valley restaurant in 2012. It was the first that I remember in most detail as it happened about 3:00 a.m. and we were all sleeping. My bedroom was over the kitchen, which was a real curse as all the garlic and kitchen odors would float upstairs and stink up my clothes. I was always embarrassed and conscious of going to school with the smell of garlic all over me, although maybe I was overly concerned as I never remember anyone saying anything.

According to my brother, Peter, it was Uncle Porky who broke down the door between his apartment and ours. He was staying with us at the time, which means it was probably during the season when the dog track was open. Mom and Dad woke my brother and me and called the local fire department. I remember being ushered into an open field next to the restaurant as we watched the firemen put out the blaze. We stood there for about an hour watching the blaze in the humid, otherwise-dark night. According to the fire department, someone had not turned off a Frialator. This is a frequent cause of restaurant fires. It was terrifying for the young kids as well as for our parents and from that time forward, I was always on a mission to move out of the upstairs into a "normal house." Mom and Dad never saw it my way, although, after a while, they certainly could have afforded to move.

After the fire, the restaurant was closed to repair the kitchen. During the course of the frightening event, I lost my favorite ring with rubies and small diamonds that was given to me by Joni, a favorite waitress. I never knew where I lost it. Several years later, my brother and I were playing in the field and I found it, picked it up, and held it up to kiss it. All I could smell was the fire that had occurred years before. It brought back terrifying memories. I still have the ring today. Whenever I see it, I am reminded of the gift of many years of life we received. The story could have ended differently if we had been overcome by smoke. Thankfully…

Left to right: Dick Gays, Mom, Dad, and Uncle Porky with me, circa 1957.

Orange, Connecticut

The summer after second grade in 1955, I was eight years old. That was the summer of having lived in Florida for almost two years. At that time my parents decided to close the restaurant for six months — the off-season — and work for my Uncle Porky, who at the time was opening a Manero's Steak House in Orange, Connecticut.

The summers were deadly and Mom and Dad knew they could not make it through another summer season so the opportunity to help Uncle Porky for about six months in the opening and establishing his restaurant was a blessing. After school got out in May, we left Hallandale in one of our station wagons, for sure a Chevy, as Dad never wanted to give the impression he had "made it" (and to be sure, he hadn't yet) and headed for our temporary digs in Stratford, Connecticut.

I don't remember too much about that summer except for two things. First, Uncle Porky was lots of fun. He had a "joie de vivre." Everyone loved him. He had a pudgy stomach thus the name, Porky, which he actually encouraged. The second thing I remember was that around the time my brother, Peter, and I entered public school for two months we had a terrible hurricane. Imagine living in Florida and expecting hurricanes to hit only to move to Connecticut to encounter Hurricane Diane there instead. The rainfall peaked at 16.86 inches and dams and rivers flooded. Many people died, hundreds of homes were destroyed, cemeteries were compromised, and open coffins and bodies floated over the streets. It was frightening and it took a couple of weeks before some normalcy returned to the area.

That summer was the first and last time we ever closed the Hallandale restaurant. Things got better when we returned and by the 1960s, after the new bridge was built and The Diplomat Hotel opened, we were on our way to being a viable business.

Porky spent a lot of time with us in the winters of my younger years. He actually spent a lot of time at the Hollywood Dog Track, which might have been one of the reasons that my parents felt we were blessedly bailed out when years later he married Florence Fitzgerald Taylor, a beautiful, wealthy widow, who had a great influence on his life as well as mine.

Porky was a charmer and had many friends in the world of entertainment, some of whom he met while in Hollywood, California years before. He was good friends with Perry Como, a well-known TV personality and entertainer of the time, with whom he had many a rollicking time. Uncle Porky continued to be a lovable presence throughout our lives until he died in 1976. He was my mom's second oldest brother, which in the Italian family put him in front of all the sisters but still in second place to Nick, a fact of history that he always seemed to challenge. The rivalry between them continued to be a strong undercurrent throughout their lifetimes and Mom, the peacemaker, was always writing letters to one or the other encouraging them to settle some disagreement or another.

Years later, after my first year of college, I spent the summer living with Uncle Porky and his wife, Florence, while working at their restaurant in Westport. Uncle Porky had long since sold the restaurant in Orange and now owned a restaurant near the town's drawbridge in Westport, Connecticut. I have many fond memories of this restaurant because it was there that I met and fell in love with my first husband, John, to whom I was introduced by Aunt Florence. The Manero's in Westport existed long after Porky died. It finally closed in the early 1990s.

Dick Gays, Manager of Manero's

Over the course of my life, our family businesses have been blessed by many great coworkers and a few extraordinary ones. Enter Dick Gays. The first picture I have of Dick's family and ours dates back to about 1956. I suspect that it was taken soon after Dick began working at the restaurant. It was about then that business began to improve and my parents would've needed more permanent help other than the short-term people who came down earlier from Connecticut.

Dick Gays and Dad met while both were working for my Uncle Nick in Greenwich. A few years later, Dick Gays started working at Manero's in Hallandale as a waiter, after closing his small sandwich shop in Hollywood, Florida. Soon after, his wife, Emily, joined him at the restaurant. My dad was aware of Dick's skills and respected him for his work ethic and honesty.

Dick was about as different from my dad as one can imagine. Although my dad was a student of the Book of Proverbs believing that "a soft answer turneth away wrath," Dick was more of the "if you can't take the heat, get out of the kitchen" school. He had a crew cut, was businesslike and serious, and after a unique religious conversion, a teetotaler. He became a dedicated Catholic Christian. He had three sons at the time, Wann, Rich, and Rob (a fourth, Dennis, to come later) and a beautiful blonde wife, Emily, who came along to help us. My brother, Peter, got to spend a lot of overnights at their house. I loved Emily, Dick, and their family but I was always envious of the fact that Peter got to spend the night and I did not — the benefits of being a male in the '50s.

The Gays family and ours with Mary Myder.
From left to right: Dick and Emily Gays with their three sons, Wann, Rob (in front), and Rich; Mary Myder, our babysitter (in the back middle); Mom (saying cheese) and Dad with Peter and me.

Soon Dick moved up to cook and then to manager. Emily moved into an office position and the team of Ellen/Art and Emily/Dick was born. They were a great team as Dick had the ability to be serious and decisive with the employees as well as with the customers, while my dad, who disliked confrontation, had the ability to be loved by all. They both needed what the other had. Our restaurant soon became popular and by the late '50s had developed its own little "Cheers" crowd with land developers, attorneys, builders, realtors, priests, politicians, and even mobsters. Dick could handle them all.

In addition to all of this, having a trusted manager like Dick meant that Dad could play golf more frequently. This was a real gift to him. Through the years our families became the closest of friends. When Dick and Emily became parents for the last time to their son, Dennis, my mom and dad became his godparents. Years later, after both my parents died, through an accident of fate, Dennis's daughter, Emily, met and married my nephew, Peter Tiernan, Jr. They dated for several weeks before they ever realized this connection. So…my parents' godson's daughter married my parents' grandson — a match made in heaven.

Hurricane Donna

In the fall of 1960, South Florida was visited by Hurricane Donna. As a child, I was secretly delighted to have a hurricane in my name. (In the years that have convened at least one or more persons, mostly my kids, have used "Hurricane Donna" to describe me in a less than positive light.) Since we had been used to many tropical depressions in South Florida, my parents made the decision to tighten up the rafters and hang on during this hurricane. After all, our building was cement and able to withstand the wind and rain. We were located on the intracoastal about two blocks from the ocean, and at the time, were not concerned about the tides.

That night our family of four went to bed, at least my brother and I did, knowing that the storm would be hitting in the middle of the night. Right on track about 2:00 a.m., the maelstrom broke with rains like gun pellets. The fear factor went from about two to ten very quickly and even more so when the steel panels which decorated the two-story building on one side were ripped off and fell to the ground with a huge deafening crash, first one and then another. It was terrifying and I remember praying to every saint I had ever heard about from the wonderful Dominican nuns who taught at our school. The hurricane persisted for many hours, and then the eye of the storm with the calm arrived. Before long, though, it picked up again ripping out trees and shrubs and sending another panel crashing to the ground invoking more fear. It was one of the scariest nights of our lives. It took the restaurant staff a few days to repair things so we could reopen, and within four days, we had electricity, water, and customers once again.

We had learned our hurricane lesson and never stayed around again to face the storms. I remember at least three trips inland to Lake Wales, Florida in the following years. My parents were not going to go through something like that again if it could be avoided. Nor did my husband, John, and I ever stay around for hurricanes in West Palm Beach when we had our family of four children, except for one time that we hunkered down in our building on Palm Beach Lakes Boulevard during a storm, which we did not expect to be that bad. We preferred to move inland and let the elements have their way without us.

Anything Can Be Corrected with Two Steak Dinners

My mom was a generous woman and gave freely of her time, talents, and resources. One of the resources she gave frequently was two steak dinners, which I supposed were then valued at about sixteen dollars when all was said and done. She would give the dinners to local community groups for fundraisers, to schools, churches, and synagogues and to anyone whom she wished to thank. She also would give them to anyone she felt she harmed in any way, kind of as an "I'm sorry" gift.

Enter Tony the painter. Things were going along better businesswise, so Mom decided to have the whole upstairs painted as part of one of many renovations. Mom hired a lovely, quiet, Italian man, Tony, who spoke very little English. It was not a particular problem as Mom spoke Italian fairly well. So Tony, who was very neat, showed up each day, removed his shoes just inside the door and started working. He did fantastic work.

After a full workday, Tony was preparing to leave when he realized that he couldn't find his shoes. These were the days when most people had their good shoes, their sneakers, and their beach shoes. These were Tony's good shoes, which is why he removed them. When he asked Mom whether she placed his shoes in an out-of-the-way spot, she said "no" but began looking. It did not take long to find out that our beloved dog, Candy, had taken a real liking to Tony's new shoes. When Mom found them, they were shredded like minced meat.

Mom's solution was a steak dinner for two. Perfect compensation. After all, she figured new shoes then were probably worth about sixteen dollars as were the two steak dinners. When I heard her plan (she just did not get it that this would not be fair compensation), I quickly called my dad, knowing this poor painter needed shoes a lot more than he needed two steak dinners. I requested Dad to come upstairs with some money for the painter, which he quickly did. The painter was happy with the money to buy new shoes *and* with a certificate for steak dinners for two.

Uncle Nick (second from left) and Dad
(on far right) with two golfing friends.

Golf

It was on the golf courses of South Florida in the 1950s, '60s, and '70s that Arthur Tiernan found customers as well as friends. Though he became engrossed as a business owner and operator, his love of golf did not dissipate; in fact, it was his way of promoting the restaurant and developing a core of friends who were crazy about him. Dad worked hard but frequently in those early years he would still find a way around lunchtime for nine holes of golf at Orangebrook, Dania, or later, when it was built, at The Diplomat.

Over the years he played with many pros such as Cary Middlecoff and Bob Murphy, as well as athletes, entertainers, and others like Mickey Mantle, Jackie Gleason, etc. Dad was extremely well liked. He would do anything for anyone. His motto was always that you "get a lot more with honey than vinegar." I never remember going out to eat with Dad at another restaurant without him running into a customer of ours and picking up their check. This little habit along with many others served him well as it wasn't long before the restaurant in Florida became successful. It was a sad day when he was on the golf course in his early '80s, hit a ball, and could not follow it because of an eye problem, later diagnosed as macular degeneration.

My dad and the restaurant sponsored many golf tournaments for a variety of causes, mostly the South Florida Kidney Association. Dad's name was well known around South Florida with golfers, because in part, of these tournaments. Later when John and I opened up in West Palm Beach we too began the same process until it just got too busy to run them anymore. Golf was good to Dad. For him, it was a way of connecting his old world with the new and helped him become the true one-of-a-kind gentleman that he was.

Dad taught both Peter and me how to play golf and we enjoyed many hours together. In high school, thanks to Dad's coaching, I had the second place on the golf team. Although I never developed the skill as he did, it was a wonderful gift to be a woman golfer in the 1960s. To this day I remember his advice: "Donna, just keep your head down," along with the saying, "tee it high and let it fly; tee it low and watch it go!"

Our family was known as a golfing family not only because of Dad's love of the sport but, of course, because of Uncle Tony Manero. Every year when the weekend of the U.S. Open is broadcast, I'll get two or three phone calls or texts letting me know that the commentators are talking about Uncle Tony on TV. When Uncle Tony and Aunt Agnes came down to Florida every winter, my dad would spend as much time on the golf course as possible with Tony, friends, and customers. Meanwhile I was in my glory because I was able to spend time with Aunt Agnes, a life-giving presence in my younger years.

The Restaurant and Lounge in Hallandale

By the late '50s, things were picking up and by the early '60s, success was on the horizon, enough so that Mom and Dad were encouraging Peter and me to go to college at some good schools "back East." They were convinced that the Northeast was the only place that "good schools" existed. If we chose to do that, they insisted, we wouldn't have to be in

Seduced by Gorgonzola

the restaurant business for the rest of our lives (ho, ho — life has a way of doing strange things).

In the 1960s, the restaurant often had a long line out the door on weekends. Oftentimes the bar was packed three-deep, according to Ed Plaisted, a South Florida *SunTimes* columnist who wrote in "Memories of Happy Nights at Manero's":

> Then there was my favorite waiter, Jerry Petrizzi, a World War II tail gunner, who controlled access to the lounge like it was the White House. Jerry, an ardent golfer, made no secret of his feelings for a customer. He never met a cheap tipper that he liked.
>
> To be admitted to Jerry's bar on the weekend was a privilege that put you in with the movers, shakers, and stars...
>
> The joint sizzled with sports stars during the season. They came from pro sports such as the Dolphins, Yankees, and Orioles in spring training at Gulfstream Park. It was popular with flight attendants from National and Eastern Airlines, a fact that attracted large male audiences to the bar.

A renovated Manero's of Hallandale in the 1970s.
Dad is in hat and Dick Gays with apron.

In addition to the above, we had the regulars. Seated at the bar almost every day would be *Gabby*, a sweet, likable, brilliant, older man who enjoyed his Glenlivet Scotch. His company developed a large area of Hallandale including wealthy residential communities near the restaurant. He lived in one of them with his lovely wife and family. Gabby was always surrounded by his team of men: builders, attorneys, laborers, insurance agents, and a variety of secretaries and support staff who would help him celebrate his company's many outstanding accomplishments.

Years later, his son, *Butch*, followed his footsteps joining him at the bar. I remember the son well for soon after being married and temporarily living in Hallandale, my husband, John, asked Butch's wife, when her baby was due. It did not go over well with the husband as the baby had been born six weeks earlier. This turned out to be one of the personal questions that John never again asked a woman.

Another of the bar crowd was led by *Bill Rooney*. Bill, a local insurance agent who was active in the Democratic Party, often brought along his staff and associates. The Rooney group loved our dividend drinks. The bar would rock when Bill Rooney was around as he was connected to everyone. He would bring in big groups who would completely take over the bar and the overflow would have to be seated in a small private room. They were good for at least a two to three hour stint. Often they would come in for a late lunch and stay for dinner and beyond.

A local hospital administrator would often come with support staff and a few physicians. Hopefully, the doctors were not on call as the custom of the day was our dividend martini with a second for good measure. Watching them taught me a lot about thoroughly checking out your doctor's history and never letting a doctor operate on you after early afternoon.

Then there was the local mayor, *Matty*, with his administrative assistant and the head of the utility department. Between these groups, I remember a lot of deal making but then I did not know what constituted a "deal." Dad said it was important not to bother any of these people, but whenever my brother and I traipsed through the lounge, all of them would dote on us by tapping our heads or taking time to stop us and talk to us as we came home from school. It was our habit to see Dad around three o'clock each day.

About the time that Peter and I would come home from school, the lunch shift of several waitresses would be leaving and the dinner crew would be moving in. Often we did our homework in the office and sometimes we'd go up and get changed and come back down. It was great fun, and looking back a lot more exciting than living in a "normal" home. It also instilled in me a lifelong desire to have a lot of people around me. On a typical evening in the early '60s (both my brother and I were old enough by this time to be hanging around the restaurant without it looking "bad") my brother Peter would work in the salad department and I would often work as the cashier. If not working, we'd hang around and visit customers all of whom seemed to enjoy the presence of older children, if only for a few minutes. In the corner booth was *Wolfie*, owner of a large drug company in Chicago. Dad used to call him "Wolf." He and his wife were always bickering about something so we did not hang around there long. The fights were legendary, prompted, I am sure, by the alcohol consumption. In spite of this, my mom and dad thought them to be quite interesting and they became friends. One year my mom and dad, both of whom enjoyed and made several car trips across the country, commandeered Wolfie's big black Cadillac back up to Chicago for them and they found it loaded with cheap cigarettes and Cuban cigars. At one stage during the trip, Dad reached down on the floor for a pencil and found a fully loaded revolver. Dad did not like guns, but after all, Wolfie and his wife were from Chicago.

Locals, Hilda and Larry Nataline, might be in the next booth. Both were friends with Mom and Dad and spent a lot of time at the restaurant. Larry was a local Sears and Roebuck salesperson and Hilda was a capable executive secretary. It was Larry who got Dad involved in the Lions Club, which had meetings and several great parties at Manero's for more than twenty years. We took many trips with the Nataline family. I especially remember one to Toronto for a convention. Years later when Mom and Dad retired to Waynesville, North Carolina, the Natalines also bought a retirement home there. One of their four children Mary Jo, now retired herself, writes:

> As I was growing up in Hallandale, one of my family's favorite places to dine was a steak house called Manero's

known for their delicious food. When I became of legal drinking age and returned to the area after nursing school, my favorite thing to do was to go to Manero's and order a whiskey sour from Frank, the bartender. Frankie would make me the best whiskey sour and fill it up with orange pieces and cherries on a stick. My parents were special friends with the owners of Manero's, Art and Ellen Tiernan, so I had an "in" with Frankie, the fruit man, as he became known to me. Every time we entered the bar area of the restaurant I would call out to Frankie; he would get this funny grin on his face and would know immediately what I was going to order. I loved seeing his look of delight and mischief as he delivered my drink. After all these many years, I have never forgotten the fun of those visits to Manero's.

The locals loved our bar because you never knew who would show up. Typically at the next table there may be some big celebrity sent over from The Diplomat Hotel, affectionately called the "Dip" by my dad. The Diplomat was opened by Sam Friedlander in 1958 on South Ocean Drive on Hallandale Beach, just north of Hallandale Beach Boulevard. Its presence in our area changed everything for our business. Dad knew all the people at The Diplomat, from the valets to the owners, and so when someone asked for a recommendation, it was to Manero's they were sent. Often when some big celebrity was in town performing, they'd come to our place to eat. It was not uncommon to see people like Walter Winchell, Larry King, Joan Rivers, Robert Goulet, Diana Shore, and others sitting in the lounge and perhaps chugging down a few Manhattans, martinis, or whiskey sours and a large steak before their show, performance, or gig. The Diplomat hosted just about every famous entertainer of the time including, Lawrence Welk, Arthur Godfrey, Frank Sinatra, Judy Garland, Jayne Mansfield, Sammy Davis Jr., Liza Minnelli, and a host of others. Most of them were our guests as well. It was a special time.

My son, Rick, tells me that Dad used to tell him stories of entertainers, long gone, who were also involved with the mob and who used to play at The Diplomat. Dad never told me of these things as I'm sure he knew it would have frightened me to death. We used to send over take-out meals (on china plates) to at least one of these entertainers. One night before he went on, he apparently was not happy with his situation or his girlfriend or something that was happening (it couldn't have been the meal) and was seen throwing our plates out of the penthouse of the several story hotel.

I didn't know it at the time (and looking back am glad I didn't) but was told much later that on more than one occasion we hosted Mafia families at the restaurant. Had I known I'd have been constantly on my knees. I was petrified by the stories of some garbage companies and the linen companies, thinking they might threaten my beloved dad. He had a gentle way with everyone though and as far as I know, no one ever strong-armed him.

On Sunday nights at Manero's, the bar would be filled with throngs of people and two diametrically opposed groups hunkering down and vying for the same space. In one corner there would be three or four tables of mostly Irish priests. The leadership of the Catholic Church would come in droves, especially on Sunday nights after their church responsibilities were over. And so it was frequent back then to see eight or ten priests with their beers, bourbons, scotch, or Irish whiskey.

They would come in after saying the last Mass or visiting with their CYO (Catholic Youth Organization) groups. They would come together in support of each other and usually to unite in word, but not usually in deed, against the local bishop. Columnist A. J. Liebling writes: "If you run across a restaurant where you often see priests eating with priests or sporting girls eating with sporting girls, you may be confident that it is good. Those are two classes of people who like to eat well and get their money's worth." That was Manero's.

These Irish priests were a tight group of mostly good and dedicated men, some of whom had a penchant for the drink in which they would indulge themselves after saying five or six Masses on Sundays for thousands of churchgoers. South Florida was inundated with Irish priests then. Those born and bred in America were the outsiders. The "Irish Mafia," they would call themselves, ironic, because in a booth right next to them one could often find members of the "other" Mafia.

Many of these priests would pour out their pain to our family. Most of these men were well loved and respected by all and they too needed a place to vent. They were the people of my childhood who had a huge influence on me then which has followed me throughout my life. Their upbeat and infectious humor, their delightful and vulnerable humanity and their proximity to my family in both geography and affection was an important part of my young life. They never intimidated me. Many of them were farm boys from large families. On many occasions they would cry their hearts out to my family about their own families back home, their struggles with loneliness and the choices they had made that led them to where they were. Dad played golf with most of them, many came to our home, and on occasion, we even vacationed with them.

The Irish priests, still wearing collars in public back then, were particularly known for this ability to connect with people. Often Dad would host parties for them upstairs after the night was over. Mom knew them all well and she, not a late night person, would walk through about 9:30 p.m. and say: "Well, enjoy yourself, Fathers, I'm going to sleep now." I never knew how she got away with that except for the fact that all of them knew she had the keys to the local church and would be opening it the next morning so the local "Father" could sleep in an extra half-hour.

In any event, those men were very good to my family and me. In the mid-'80s, when I was in my late thirties, I spent five years studying theology at St. Vincent de Paul Regional Seminary in Boynton Beach, Florida and saw firsthand what constituted their discipline. Many friends could not understand why I would want to study there, but I felt completely at home and comfortable, even though there were less than a handful of women there. It was exactly what I needed at the time to develop an adult faith, and it certainly provided my life with a "road less traveled." Many of the men with whom I studied or who were my professors are among my dearest friends today. The seminary redirected the course of my life and I am most grateful. I now view the priesthood in quite a different way from the way I did back then. I see it with many positives as well as many dysfunctions that need to be corrected in order to have healthy priests and a healthy Church. (I have written about this in a book called *Touching the Face of God*.)[9] Still, I am as thankful as ever for the presence of these men in my childhood life.

Dad, Porky, Nick, and Tony, circa 1974.

Kick it, Kid

My Uncle Tony won the U.S. Open almost eighty years ago. I have some wonderful memories of Uncle Tony. He was a kindly gentleman although a stickler for doing things properly. Before John and I were to be married, it was just assumed John would become a good golfer. Actually, it was a requirement in our family. John, for some reason, played golf with his left hand although he wrote with his right (he was probably a natural lefty and switched by the nuns when he was younger). When we were dating, my dad did all he could to educate John in the game of golf and John eventually became a decent golfer, squeezing in a game whenever my dad invited him or when he had time. Before we were married in 1968, his golfing skills were given an upgrade when Uncle Tony encouraged him to play right-handed and gave him a few lessons. The lessons were put to the test when we were playing with Dad and Uncle Tony one Saturday morning at the Dania Golf Course just north of Hollywood.

I was a little nervous when playing with Uncle Tony. I was always encouraged to play from the men's tee so I teed off first. I had a decent drive down the middle, about a hundred eighty yards out and reasonably placed. Then Uncle Tony and Dad teed off, far surpassing me of course, which was to be expected. Finally came John, who stood up, addressed the ball, took a deep breath, and swung. Nervous to be playing with the master, he completely missed the ball. Uncle Tony, seeing his embarrassment, immediately said, "Just relax and try again."

John took another deep breath, stood up straight, adjusted his stance, and swung a second time. He missed again. About that time, someone standing in the foursome behind us yelled out, to our great embarrassment: "Just kick it, kid." Dad encouraged John to pick up the ball and move on to where we all had our second shot. John (not one to be defeated in anything) completely dejected, picked up the ball, jumped into the cart, and drove down the course. That was one of those stories we all told for years whenever we needed to put him back in his place.

Rich Gays, Manager

Rich Gays, previously mentioned, was one of my childhood loves and a lifelong friend. He had the opportunity to work with my dad and became assistant manager in 1970. John and I were married at the time and had moved north to operate our own restaurant in West Palm Beach. Rich spent twenty-five years working with my dad at Manero's in Hallandale. Dad loved and trusted Rich like a son. Rich has wonderful stories, told with an Irish wit, which could be another book. He completely managed the restaurant after his dad, Dick, died of cancer and my parents had retired. I am grateful to him for reviving and adding to some of my childhood memories.

He reminded me of the people who would come for lunch Monday through Friday and do their "business" over drinks until about 3:00 p.m. when they would leave to go home to their families or be picked up by their wives. Oftentimes the staff would drive one or more of them home. They would come because they knew that it was comfortable and safe and with the knowledge that the staff and management would take care of them. Manero's was friendly, had great food, dividend drinks, and a staff of great bartenders. There was Louie, the hairdresser from New Jersey, who would do night duty as a bartender. Then we had Frankie from Brooklyn who would greet the customers with a big "how war ya?" Jackie, the elder, was another of these wonderful characters who often would scratch his glasses to get the dirt away only to realize there was no glass there. This was a unique group of regular guys, all with their idiosyncrasies, which made them lovable to patrons. They were some of the many reasons that restaurant attracted many famous and infamous people. When the moon was full, Manero's would rock with crazies. (Say what you want but I'd bet my life on the full moon theory.)

A rare gathering of the clan.
Dad, Peter (my brother), Uncle Porky, me, Uncle Nick, Mom, and John.

According to Richie, to be seen in the bar and the lounge frequently were: The Gibbs brothers; Danny Thomas, who always requested a fried egg sandwich; Gabby Hayes, when he wasn't filming; Steve Lawrence and Eydie Gorme; Diana Shore; Joan Rivers; news commentators from Miami including at the time, Larry King; Archbishop McCarthy from Miami; and Donald Trump before he was known as "The Donald." Richie relates:

> One day in the early '60s we got a call that President Kennedy would be coming. In no time, the restaurant

was full of FBI agents who were there to check out the place. Prior to Kennedy's arrival, they requested a list of employees. The staff had become quite familiar with the FBI who frequently trailed some of our more questionnable customers. After we gave the FBI the list of employees, they reported back to us that some people would not be allowed to come to work that day and they told us exactly who those employees were. We reworked the schedule to remove those people for that day. As it turned out, the President was diverted by other business and would not be coming for dinner. Since these were the days before we could check out employees on the internet it left questions forevermore in our minds about those staff persons who were going to be told not to report to work.

Sitting with Rich for a few hours and listening to stories of princes and paupers, bartenders and lawyers, priests and mobsters, entertainers and chefs, is one of the most entertaining experiences one could wish to have. Rich tells stories of the man who came out of the restroom and complained that another customer had peed on him. Other tales included the humorous waiter who was told by a customer that there was a fly in his soup to which he responded: "Shush, this is Hallandale, everyone will want one." He tells of the well-known men in the community who would come with their "nieces" or their "nephews," and the doctors, who, along with the owners of the race track, the wealthiest of the well-off in that little town, who were, according to Rich, the absolute worst tippers.

He also related that my dad, who had a policy of not cashing third party checks, taught him one of the best lessons of his life when he made him go down and request payment from a mobster who had bounced a check on us that Rich had cashed.

All restaurants are unique, but Manero's in Hallandale, indeed, was a mixture of the greatest characters. "Hear no evil; see no evil" seemed to be the unspoken motto.

Retirement

My parents retired from the restaurant business in 1978 and a couple of years later, Uncle Nick died. I was shocked when they said they were going to retire, as the restaurant business was so much a part of their lives. Manero's in Hallandale continued to thrive under the capable management of Rich Gays who then worked for my cousins, especially Nick Manero, Jr. By this time, John and I were totally involved in our business in West Palm Beach and my beloved brother Peter, who had long since graduated from Villanova and then the University of Florida with a degree in law, was soon to be operating another Manero's in Margate, while practicing law on the side. I'm not sure how you do that but Peter is extremely bright, reads voraciously, writes prolifically in law magazines, and is a hard worker. He continued in Margate until 1993 when he went back to law full time. At last, my parents would be happy that at least one of us got out.

Mom upon being awarded Woman of the
Year by the Chamber of Commerce.

Memories

Some other of my fondest memories include:

Bringing my father a clean dry shirt every evening about 7:00 p.m.;

Drying silverware on busy nights;

Smelling of Gorgonzola salad forever (why I never even ate it until I was forty-five);

My Italian uncles who always jokingly used the phrase: "baccia galupe," which poorly translated means "kiss my butt";

Meeting endless customers and learning to look them in the eye, and shake their hands and smile (and me being terribly uncomfortable just as some of my grandchildren are now);

My dad's famous oriental phrase: "walls have ears" which I now understand he used so freely with the variety of people frequenting the restaurant;

Endless nights of falling asleep in a booth in the bar;

My mother and her "Cruella de Ville" glasses;

Looking out my bedroom window and trying to figure out what those noisy people were doing in their cars below;

Hand washing glasses in the morning with my dad with the smell of wine and alcohol all over the bar;

Crushes on endless busboys, waiters, and kitchen staff with whom I spent endless hours (one of them, John Porazin, just got in touch with me last month after fifty-eight years);

Learning the customer is *almost* always right — actually I learned that they are "always right" but I have become a lot more discriminating of late;

Being taught to do the bookkeeping when I was old enough;

Learning to seat patrons in the dining room and to take the receipts;

My Italian uncles pinching me on the bottom, a sign of affection for youngsters and women which always made me uncomfortable (years later, when I traveled to Italy, I began to understand what cultural acceptance it had and I still hated it);

Hundreds of waitresses — the sisterhood we called them — who worked lunch and sometimes dinner shifts while their kids were in school (many of them still correspond with me today);

And finally, I remember admiring Dad's collection of hats from Lily Dache of New York. Nick would send them for Dad to wear. He would wear them when Nick was in town or for photographs but hated the pretense as they were just not him. Give him a golf cap any day.

Despite all of these wonderful memories I had decided in childhood that the restaurant business would definitely not be my choice. Nor would I ever marry anyone who was in the business. I saw how hard my parents worked and what sacrifices they made. I was brought up by Mom and Dad to be responsible, polite, trustworthy, and honest. These values were not always found in people in our business and often that made me quite uncomfortable. Getting out of this crazy business was not only important, it was critical. I was going to be a psychologist.

My Friends' Memories

A few months ago, I returned to a grammar school reunion, fifty-two years after eighth grade graduation. It was a joy to go back as I had nothing but delightful memories of the eight years I spent at Little Flower School in Hollywood, Florida. The Adrian Dominican nuns who taught us were fantastic and all my schoolmates were dear, close friends. I loved school, I loved learning, and I could not wait each day to get there, once I got past six-year-old fear of leaving Mom and Dad and the anxiety that they might forget to pick me up.

At the reunion, I was told time and time again by my childhood friends how much they loved coming to my home over the restaurant for overnights and parties. Apparently what I had taken for granted and sometimes hated — living over the restaurant — was the object of great envy and admiration of my friends. They loved going into the kitchen, digging into the desserts, and making sundaes. They loved the smell of Gorgonzola cheese and watching customers come and go. They enjoyed walking down and exploring under the drawbridge next to the restaurant. They reveled over all of the attention they received from the waiters and waitresses. Most all of them told me they couldn't wait for my birthday parties when they could order anything from the menu and run around the restaurant like they owned it. Here all the time all

I wanted was a "normal home" and they would have given their eyeteeth to have what I had. The grass *is* always greener…

Growing Up in Two Worlds

Looking back I really grew up in two worlds in the 1950s. I grew up in the church world, my mom being a strict Catholic and following every rule to the nth degree. This was not uncommon for her time; fear of the fires of hell was a dominating factor in controlling people's lives and loves in the Church. Dad went along with my mom in her religious decisions but lacked the fear factor which dominated her life. His Irish Catholicism, influenced by the Druids, made him a lot more comfortable when it came to matters of spirituality and religion. This was our saving grace for Dad always moderated whatever Mom decided. (My kids might make the same statement.) This left us somewhat grounded in reality.

The church was supported by the Catholic school system, which at the time, was superb. I was a good student and followed all the rules. Life was a lot easier back then if you followed the rules. Because I did this I was a favorite among most of my teachers and do not have a lot of the unhappy stories often told by others who had the Catholic school experience. Make no mistake, fear was a huge factor in our Catholic upbringing — for a young child, the fear of hell fire for eternity was a pretty good motivation for staying on track.

On the other hand, I grew up over a restaurant. In the restaurant business you see everything. Often those things involved a seamier side of life. I was taught to make no judgments, unless of course one's behavior intruded on or threatened the well-being of one of our family, friends, employees, or guests, but…you see it all. My bedroom was located over the parking lot where late at night people would have been drinking and then cavorting in their cars. In addition there was lots of loud laughter, pranks that often looked like fun but often ended up in serious arguments. At times, there were even physical fights and we would have to call in the police.

I do not want to go into a bawdy account of what happens late night when restaurants close. But also trust me when I say, although his world is much different from ours, Anthony Bourdain was not greatly exaggerating when he wrote some of his accounts. The restaurant business, like any business today, can be very base. Many restaurant people live close to the edge. Many are in a transitional time of their lives where they are trying to figure it all out. Although we didn't have the proliferous drugs that exist today, we had plenty of seedy characters whom we came across and with whom we had to deal.

Hallandale, at the northern end of Miami, was home to many cultures in a variety of businesses, licit and illicit. It was a difficult task to know who to treat gingerly, who to befriend and support, and who to invite to your house parties. Let's just say, the restaurant business was about as far removed from the church world back then as a young child can imagine.

After my years of theological education, I was able to recognize that our family business is and was what theologians and sociologists would call a "sitz im leben," a German phrase meaning a place where the rubber hits the road, where life, with all its good and bad, takes place. It's also a place where God, however you understand that Great Energy Force, exists. The important thing is to be a positive influence wherever you are; do the best you can wherever you are and raise the standards of whatever business in which you are involved.

In trying to reconcile a somewhat unhealthy business with my family values, I began to recognize over the years that our mission was to live our values as best as we could. Those we came into contact with could either learn from the way we did business or think us out of touch with restaurant reality. As our beloved Pope Francis displays in all his words and deeds: accept all, judge none.

Growing up, I was always embarrassed a little by being in a business known for having an element of employees who wanted to be paid under the table, cheat on their taxes, or steal from their employers. I was also infuriated by owners who would put up with or even encourage those things. They offended the way my parents brought me up. Those things were rampant in the restaurant business. In some corners, they still are. As humorous as I find the exploits of some restaurateurs and restaurant workers, I generally find that people in our business are capable of great generosity and kindness. For every one of these people who gives our business a bad name, there are many others who exemplify goodness, compassion, humanity, and integrity.

Donna Tiernan Mahoney

Manero's of Hallandale

The second time I saw one of Manero's restaurants destroyed (the Hallandale restaurant), I thought I would throw up in grief. It was knocked down in 2004 (currently a 33-story condo is being built on the property), not many years after I had already witnessed the horrifying destruction of our West Palm Beach restaurant.

Once the Hallandale restaurant was gone I realized that I could never go back and visit my childhood home. It was not only the business that made my family's lives possible, but it was our family home. It held the memories of my youth. It represented love and friends and good times and bad times and my parents, both of whom are now gone; Mom died in 2001 and Dad in 2006. It represented my mom's family, and visits from both families, including my cousins, Bob and Dick Manero, Johnny Costaregni, Nick and Lita Manero, Joe Tiernan, and Susan Fruzen, all of whose presences I craved. It represented literally millions of meals served and friends made and hopes and dreams spoken about. It held memories of fires and stress, hurricanes and land crabs, sleepovers and parties.

Me with my brand new "Huffy" and Peter in
the background in his cowboy outfit
and the first of many of our delivery trucks.

This is where Peter and I played cowboys and Indians and where I rode my first bike. It was the place from which I left to go to school in the mornings and where my family huddled together in the fright of the Cuban Missile Crisis and later, where we came together at the death of John F. Kennedy. Here was where my friends stayed before my wedding to John and where we brought home our first baby. These and millions more happy memories for me were at 2600 East Hallandale Beach Boulevard and now it was nothing but empty space.

Thomas Wolfe said it well when he wrote: "You can't go home again." I now know that I carry all these memories and they are part of me. I no longer need a physical place to which I might return. But still, to see this place in which I grew up reduced to an empty space was an incredible life lesson: It's not the place that's important — it's the people, relationships, and memories of love which are ours for a lifetime. Manero's of Hallandale provided thousands of those wonderful memories for many people. No one can destroy those for any of us. It was, simply put, just a wonderful childhood.

You don't choose the day you enter the world and you don't choose the day you leave. It's what you do in between that makes the difference.
—Anita Septimus

CHAPTER THREE

Manero's in West Palm Beach, Florida

Humbling Beginnings

All through our courtship, I heard John talk about the Cattleman's Restaurant, located at East 45th Street in New York City. His mother's friend, Everett Massoletti, a restaurateur in New York, always told John he'd give him a great recommendation should he want to work there. Everett's father had been a famous restaurateur and President of the NYC Restaurant Association years before and Everett was like some second-generation success stories that did not quite get the whole picture of what it meant to really work. In spite of that, he was a good and kindly man. Years later, John, who always remembered a kindness, cared for him when he became destitute. John gave him a job and watched out for him until the day he was struck and killed by an automobile in front of our restaurant in West Palm Beach. It was quite sad, but in his last few years, Everett was well taken care of by John and that was a blessing.

Before we were married in 1968, John interviewed at the Cattleman Restaurant, one of New York's finest. John had extensive restaurant training, having chosen to go to a technical school for the basics as well as having done restaurant work since the age of fourteen. Later he returned to college to learn the business side of restaurant management. While he was studying for his economics degree he worked at Manero's Restaurant in Westport where I met him in the summer of 1965. He had worked in many upscale restaurants before Manero's and had many hilarious stories of his own to share as well as considerable experience in proper management.

At Manero's, he did it all. He could tend bar, work the kitchen, and operate the floor. My Aunt Florence and Uncle Porky were delighted to have him because he was so versatile. When they introduced us the summer before I began college, they told me stories of his work ethic. A year later when I spent the summer with them, they encouraged our dating. Our first date was a barbecue at my aunt's club in Millerton, New York. She set the whole thing up. She told me he was a fine young man and was related to the Maher Brothers who started a big business in Greenwich, ironically, across from the first Manero's. In addition, when Uncle Porky was young, John's father, Maher Mahoney, and he used to hang out together. A blissful two-year courtship began while both of us were in college.

John was given many extraordinary recommendations both by my aunt and uncle as well as other people for whom he worked. I have come across some of them in recent years and they warm my heart. Needless to say, when this eager and hard-working young man showed up at the Cattleman, they grabbed him immediately.

The week we returned from our incredible Bermuda honeymoon in July of 1968, complete with suntans, high expectations, and saturated with Mateus Rose, we settled into our small apartment in Rye, New York. John had just graduated before we were married, but I still had one year to go. I began summer classes at Manhattanville College, thinking it would lighten my load during my last year before graduation. I now had housekeeping duties that would take some time. (Back then these things were important.) It was a good plan because by mid-September, I was pregnant with our first son, Jay, and it would have been challenging to be on campus all day long while my body was adjusting to this new and blessed reality.

John began his morning trek into New York City. I would drive him to the Rye station, which was close by. He was stunning (and maybe a little strange) all dressed up in a $150 tuxedo at seven in the morning. Looking like a million dollars, he would arrive at the Cattleman and begin his daily routine. He worked two shifts — lunch and dinner — and returned home in the evening around midnight, six days a week. He did everything at the Cattleman, but mostly he served as maître d'. He would come home with incredible stories that sustained us for weeks. These were the days of heavy union activity in the restaurant business and he told me what he felt I could handle. John shielded me from a lot, I am sure.

After a long week, which seemed like a month, it was obvious to both of us that this was not a good way to start a marriage. John was exhausted after the third day and the only time I saw him was when I drove him into the station. On Sunday following the first week, sensing that it was not going to get better, we had a serious talk during which we both agreed that he should find other employment. That evening he called in and said he was giving his two-week notice. They were not happy. Actually the head maître d' was irate and told him not to come in at all. John requested that they put his hundred dollars pay in the mail and he was told to call the office in the morning. The next day he was told that a check would be sent to him. A hundred dollars does not sound like much now, but in 1968 our weekly food budget was twenty dollars. One hundred dollars was a lot of money back then.

We waited and waited for the check as now he was jobless and I was in school. The check never came so he was out the hundred dollars salary and had a slightly used tuxedo worth $150 in his possession. I don't remember him ever using it again. The experience was a good one as it taught us how not to treat employees. Life went on and within a few weeks he got a job as a real estate research associate for a gentleman who did a lot of investing in Putnam and Westchester Counties. He knew this would not be permanent as, unknown to me at the time, my worst fears were coming true. He and my dad (who was crazy about John) had been plotting to open a Manero's Restaurant in West Palm Beach. I never figured out how all this happened without my knowing it. I was in school finishing my psychology degree. I was pregnant, tired, and in love. Somehow, this plot took place between my beloved father and my beloved husband right in front of my eyes.

The story unfolds. The year went by; I graduated in 1969, and we made the trek to Florida with my parents in my car, and John and me in his Volvo. Mom and Dad had come north for my graduation and to help us as they were convinced that I was going to deliver our son, Jay, on highway I-95 on the trip back to Florida. Thankfully, he was born three weeks later when we were comfortably ensconced at my parents' home in Hallandale. While I was madly in love with our new son, John Arthur (Jay), and was busy changing diapers, John and Dad began looking at property in West Palm Beach.

In years to come I would often tease John that he married me for the Manero's name and the opportunity to be in the restaurant business. By the time John was growing up, Manero's had made a name for itself in the area. Unquestionably, he would have made it without the Manero's name as he believed that customer service was an attitude one breathed, but still, I believe there was at least a touch of truth in my teasing accusations.

The construction of the property in West Palm Beach: John and me with baby, Jay, and two of Dad's golfing friends including "Lit" Sicliano (far right), and an unidentified professional golfer.

The Opening of West Palm Beach

We opened the restaurant in August of 1970. The property was bought in 1969 by the Hallandale Corporation. It had been planned by John and Dad together with the help of a brilliant architect from Palm Beach, John Stetson. Its style was Mediterranean with a Mexican tile red roof. It was a stately building with lovely lines erected on the corner of Palm Beach Lakes Boulevard and Spencer Drive. At the time, except for a nursing home, we were one of the few buildings on the street. Highway I-95 was not yet complete, but we knew it was coming soon. The restaurant was built by R. S. Black, a local West Palm Beach builder. They spared no cost to make it exactly what was wanted and needed, unlike our previous restaurant in Hallandale. We were delighted with the outcome and excited to start our new business, which was actually owned by Mom, Dad, and Uncle Nick, but we hoped that someday we would purchase it from them.

Meanwhile, John and I had a contract to move into brand new digs at the Granada apartments on nearby Congress Avenue but a fire occurred in the development and slowed it down about six months. That meant that each day John commuted an hour each way from Hallandale. Just before the restaurant's grand opening, we were able to move into our own apartment. It was hotter than blazes on that wonderful, celebratory August night in West Palm Beach that year we opened the new Manero's, and to me felt like at least 100 degrees. I was once again pregnant with a very big baby.

Seduced by Gorgonzola

A celebration during construction phase in West Palm Beach: Tony Manero, Rick Black (builder), Dad, John Stetson (architect), and John; February, 1970.

Harold Hill

A few weeks before we opened we started the hiring. I will never forget the day in July 1970 when Harold Hill walked into the office. He was about 5'2" short, stocky, with a kind of flattop haircut. He had a brusque businesslike manner, which I interpreted as rude. Now I realize it was his way of handling his nervousness. He had just retired from a full-time job and said he wanted part-time work as a bookkeeper/accountant. I was twenty-three and John was twenty-seven, just beginning the biggest venture of our lives. I remember thinking in my inexperienced mind why in the world would we hire this old man (he was my current age). What could he possibly do for us?

There were three of us in the office, John and I, and a forty-year-old secretary named *Jean*. Jean, although delightful, spent most of the day fixing her hair and make-up. She was kind of like Tim Conroy's "Ms. Wiggins" but very attractive. She had been hired to do the office work but would probably have admitted that she was there looking for a man to replace her husband, an attorney from whom she was divorced. That was fine as I enjoyed her entertaining commentaries and we got along well. We just assumed that the bulk of the work would be done by the three of us, but in the office, primarily by Jean and me. John would be stretched with the management of the 280-seat restaurant. In the beginning, we would get help from our "mother restaurant" in Hallandale but then it would be up to us. I was sure that the work could be done by Jean who was full time at forty hours, assisted by me on a part-time basis. I was five months pregnant and had one baby at home so full time was out of the question for me.

I worked early mornings through lunch and got most of the bookwork finished by 11:30 a.m. when I would appear as a hostess. Then I would stay until about one o'clock and take home any work to finish while our son, Jay, was napping. Workaholism had already shaped our young family and I, thinking it was normal, just fell in line. We opened the restaurant to a huge crowd of people and we were soon in the limelight of West Palm Beach. Within two weeks, we were overloaded with work, and mutually decided to look into our files to find more help. In desperation the only application we could find was that of the "long in the tooth" Harold Hill. We called him "Mr. Hill." That's what everyone called him, including John and me, for at least five years. He began working with us first in the mornings in the office and then out front as cashier as his day was extended after our second son, Patrick Richard (Rick), was born.

Mr. Hill taught me everything from bookkeeping to restaurant skills to handling the people in the Palm Beach area. "They were different," he always said. He knew all the locals. His wife took me to many of the prestigious clubs in Palm Beach for luncheons and I began networking with some of the other business people around town. Both Mr. Hill and his wife escorted me around town and introduced me to several people on some evenings while John was working. Mr. Hill was, as it turned out, a real godsend and I just hope and pray that someone, someday, will say that I have taught them half of the many skills he taught me.

He loved it when we took vacations at which time he, as senior member of the organization, could rule the roost. He was most capable of doing this. One year I remember being on vacation in Gatlinburg. This was the summer of the bicentennial, 1976, and by this time we had been blessed with our daughter, Shannon Marie, and I was recently

Seduced by Gorgonzola

pregnant with our fourth, Erin Marie, when we got a call from the restaurant saying that there had been a robbery. The robbers assaulted Mr. Hill who then sported a big bump on his head for weeks. I thought that would be the end of him, but not so. He was back and happily at work within a few days. He said that he could not stand being at home any longer. He and his second wife had somewhat of a tumultuous relationship. He probably would have worked for free.

Mr. Hill worked with us from that fall in 1970 until he was about the age of eighty, when he became ill. He was our eyes and ears when we were away — nothing got by HH, which is what we came to, affectionately, call him. He was admired by many people in the area and although I often thought him harsh and too opinionated, he steered us away from many troublesome situations. Looking back, he always sat at a makeshift desk in John's office and never complained. The desk couldn't have been any wider than two and a half feet or any deeper than about two feet. He was just happy to be able to give input. I think I thanked him many times, but just in case, I look skyward and say: "Thanks, Mr. Hill, and forgive me for the rash judgment of my youth. You were a big part of the huge success that was Manero's on Palm Beach Lakes Boulevard."

The Van with the Sign

I wish to share the inadvisability of bringing home a van with the business name on it, especially if the business deals in cash. This would never be the problem today as about 95 percent or more of our business is done by credit card. Today there is usually not enough cash from the evening receipts to pay out the employees their tips placed on credit cards. However, back in the '70s, cash was still king and most people thought restaurant people brought home cash.

We had just purchased our first home on the water (okay, it was a canal) in West Palm Beach and we were still getting settled. We had a van then with the name "Manero's" plastered all over as things were beginning to pick up. We were known by most people in the town, having been there for about a year. Those were the days when John had not yet seen the light regarding his drinking and was known to have a few "belts," as he would call them, to relax after a long day's work. A few days after we moved into our new home, John came home to our family after having had these few belts and he parked the van in the driveway, came inside, and went to bed.

About 3:00 a.m., I heard our two dogs, beautiful Hungarian Vizslas named Homer and Hugo, barking like crazy. I elbowed John to wake up but he was a heavy sleeper. After a few more strong elbows, I decided to handle the situation myself. I got up and turned on the lights. The dogs were still barking. I went out through the living room into the family room to the back sliding glass door and found it open. Someone had broken the lock. I let the dogs out the back and they went after the scent of the intruders who, by this time, must have figured out that it wasn't worthwhile tempting two large dogs. I immediately checked the boys' room, then the guest room, the rest of the house and then the garage. I turned on every single light in the house. By this time the dogs were quiet so I closed the patio door, jammed a lot of furniture against it, and returned to the still-sleeping John. In the morning I told John what happened.

It was a few weeks later that John said he thought he might join AA. He did and for the rest of his life he never looked back.

"When the student is ready, the teacher will appear."

My Sugar, Butter, and Small Accompaniment Rant

About mid-'70s, sugar prices skyrocketed — so much so that it became necessary to ration sugar to our customers. You see, we had a certain clientele who would come to the early dinner with large purses and empty the entire sugar containers into their purses. Not only sugar but at some tables, everything that was brought to the tables would be missing when the customers left. You may think I'm exaggerating. I am not. In West Palm Beach, we had to bolt everything less than two feet by three feet to the walls. Pictures, planters, and all kinds of things went missing from day to day. Pilferage was constant, and not only of sugar and butter.

But now that I've written that, let me confess, for my kids will quickly tell you the following if I do not. They would remind me that they frequently find sugar packets from McDonald's, Chic-fil-A, and Cracker Barrel in my car. Of course. I always make sure that I have one sugar for my unsweetened iced tea. I hardly consider this a confession-worthy crime. Sure, one sugar or two sugars, that's okay. But the whole bowl? Be like me — take one or maybe two — we give you permission. But don't be like the good people of a certain community in the '70s in Palm Beach County. Please don't supply your entire Equal, sugar, Sweet and Low, butter, salt-and-pepper shakers, knives, forks, and spoons as well as rock glasses and flower vases from our restaurant. Give us a little break. As the famous CNBC's Jim Kramer, recent restaurateur, will tell you: the margins today just aren't that great.

Jay, Shannon, and Rick with their aprons on, prepping for a potential future, 1974.

Sophie

In the history of every restaurant, there are always a few people who stand out. None stands out like Sophie Solof. Even the name is remarkably outlandish, isn't it? Sophie was an older woman (again, about my age now) and nothing short of an eccentric character. She was a businesswoman from Pittsburgh who inherited her family's furniture store. She was always complaining about everything, including the "crap" made today that was passed off as furniture. We knew that she was just trying to help us with her words of wisdom as she believed that being forewarned is being forearmed. We did not always accept her critique of society, being young and wide-eyed, but we patiently listened to her.

Sophie was a woman before her time. She operated in the '50s, '60s, and '70s in a man's world, but would never accept being treated as anything less than a first-class citizen. Sophie had been one of my parents' customers in Hallandale. She literally fell in love with three generations of males in our family: my dad, Arthur, whom she called Arnie; my husband John, whom she called Johnny; and our sons, Jay, whom she called JJ and Rick, whom she called Ricky. (At the time this story begins, our daughters, Shannon and Erin had not yet been born.) Sophie put up with my mother and me only because that would give her access to our men. Mom and I didn't mind. In fact, we were rather amused.

Sophie was outrageous in so many ways, a regular Auntie Mame. She had been married twice but had no use for her previous husbands. She rarely spoke about them, but frequently spoke about her dad, whom she loved. She had no children and was awkward in her dealing with them. Other than John and my parents, she was the only other one present at our oldest son Jay's birth, where she was thrown out of the hospital as she, not a quiet person, made so much noise. There used to be an old hospital sign with a nurse holding her finger in front of her mouth as if to say "shhh." Whenever I see it, I think of Sophie being thrown out of the hospital. Of course those were the days that John was drinking and my father was probably celebrating too so they might have played some part in her quick exit as well.

Sophie dressed in mismatched colors. She, a self-proclaimed "good female golfer," would frequently come in with striped shirt and checkered pants (yes, I know that works today, but back then, it didn't). In addition, I only remember seeing her real hair once as she wore straw wraps on her head in a variety of colors of aqua blue, red, yellow, and pink. She could have afforded a nice wig but chose these straw replacements instead.

Seduced by Gorgonzola

Although she had lived in Hallandale, Florida in a condo at The Diplomat for many years, she decided to move to West Palm Beach in the early '70s, soon after we did. I knew she felt secure being near her "Johnny" who would do anything for her. And in this way she could watch her "JJ" and "Ricky" grow up. She bought a condo at the Lands of the President, a few minutes from us, and showed up at the bar at the Manero's about 5:00 p.m. every evening. She always had one drink, a bourbon Manhattan. She would sit for about an hour talking to our bartender, Carlos, from Spain, whom John sponsored into the country. She got to know everyone in the bar and although she was Jewish, she told everyone she was a member of the Mahoney family. This was touching but because she was so outspoken, it was also embarrassing.

Whenever anyone, especially John, asked Sophie how it was going her answer was always the same: "Johnny, it's better not to know." In spite of all the bad things in her life she had her Tiernan/Mahoney men. She also had a man who worked for her in Pittsburgh whom she called "Little Earl." He was probably three years younger than Sophie but was still "Little Earl." Although Sophie was in our lives for about twenty years, I never met "Little Earl" but I trusted that he existed. Sophie attended all family gatherings and we came to call her Aunt Sophie, which she loved.

Sophie died in her early '80s, much too soon, but she had had enough. She couldn't put up with the world any longer. Not by accident, she checked herself into Darcy Hall, a nursing home across the street from Manero's in West Palm Beach. John would personally deliver food to her every single day. He was so good to her. Those days were very busy days for us with four young kids, both of us working at our business as well as sixty to seventy coworkers for whom we had to be present, but still, he was there visiting Sophie every day. Sophie, the outrageous, taught me the value of nonconforming, a lesson I needed to learn. She taught me patience and she taught me to love deeply those who are different from us.

I don't remember where Sophie was buried. It doesn't matter. Sophie, the outrageous, will always live on in our hearts.

Dad, Mom, me, and John celebrating the honor of
the Linda Pelka Award of Excellence.

The Palm Beach County Restaurant Award

In 1980, the Palm Beach County Restaurant Association awarded us the Linda Pelka Restaurant of the Year Award. It was a prestigious award, especially since we were competing with hundreds of fine restaurants from Boca Raton all the way to Jupiter. We were extremely honored to receive the award. The award, for me, was a mixed blessing. When we first opened Manero's in West Palm Beach, we agreed that we would give it five years to see if we could make it a success or else I would go back to school to become a practicing psychologist and John would find employment in a career that was easier on families. After the first five years, we decided that we would give it another five, which would bring us into the early eighties. When we received this award in 1980 I was both proud as a peacock, but also in a quandary as I knew that our fate had been sealed. The dream of becoming a psychologist was going to have to remain on the back burner for many years. As for John, it was the recognition by his peers that he was an outstanding restaurateur and could pretty much go anywhere he wanted. Regardless, he wanted only a career in Manero's where he could determine his own destiny. Since that time we've received many wonderful awards but none has had the impact of that one.

Two of the Many Gifts of our Business: Trudy and Walter

Everyone who walks through our restaurant doors shares their life in some way whether they know it or not. This has become more obvious to me with age. One learns to "read people" not only in what they say but in how they say it, their facial expressions, how they treat people and the way they expect to be treated. We truly carry our history with us in more ways than we know. I knew that when I first sat Trudy and Walter, a couple who came weekly to our restaurant in West Palm Beach. They were from Germany, both in their seventies when we first met them. She was a strong German woman with a beautiful face and gentle blue-green eyes. He was a smaller man, which probably had something to do with the disease from which he suffered — muscular dystrophy. Trudy would wheel Walter in each Thursday for the beef stroganoff. Within a few visits, I knew this couple would have an impact on my life and teach me many lessons. They did.

They were born around 1905 in Germany. They endured two world wars and the insipid and horrific leadership of the Nazi government before immigrating to the United States. They knew fear. They knew extremes. They knew death. They knew the art of survival and they knew how to live on practically nothing. I was reminded of all these things when I recently saw the extraordinary movie, *The Book Thief*. I thought a lot of how they, too, spent many days and nights in protected shelters as they waited for the bombing to stop. All these things they showed on their faces but mostly they showed love and courage. They had a lifetime of living through difficult situations and had become people of integrity and substance.

Within a few meetings, I knew that Trudy and Walter were sent to Manero's for more than a meal. Their presence reminded me of the many blessings of our relatively easy lives. I felt that they needed our family and a little of our activity in their lives. If there was one thing the Mahoney family had plenty of, it was activity as I encouraged the kids to "try" all kinds of sports and afterschool endeavors. Little did I know then how much we needed them to learn many lessons of courage.

As Trudy and Walter became regulars at our family celebrations, my mom and dad enjoyed them too, although their presence, I'm sure, was a reminder to Dad of the horrors of the war in which he had served. For each family event, John would go to Century Village where they lived, pick them up and then return them. He did this so that Trudy would not have to handle the wheelchair. They loved being with the kids. The place they lived was pretty much of a retirement community. We tried to include them in everything we could although Walter's disease was quite advanced.

Trudy shared much with me. In earlier days, Walter was a machinist in the North when he could work and for twenty-five years they had a decent middle-class life. When his disease progressed they felt that a move to Florida would ease some of the stress of the cold winters. We had many an iced tea together and Trudy would tell me of her fear of Walter getting too difficult for her to handle. I specifically remember one day that I went to visit her. Walter was in a nursing home on a temporary basis, but they could only afford it for a while longer and then she would have to bring him home. She gave me a figurine of a beautiful strong woman with her hands raised above her head in celebration. Trudy had brought it from Germany. I have looked it up on the internet and it is quite valuable, but the value to me is in the memory it holds of the day she gave it to me.

Soon after this I went again to visit and found her quite upset. She took me to her medicine cabinet and told me she was saving pills for when she and Walter could no longer handle it. It was at the stage that she could no longer lift him. Their plan was to bring him home and have a celebration meal. After that she would give Walter several pills and take the rest herself. I told her I did not agree with that idea. Furthermore, I never thought she'd go through with it but it had me quite troubled as, at the time, I thought of suicide as a terrible moral failing rather than an act of desperation.

I never saw Trudy or Walter at their home again. Soon after that visit I got a call from her Lutheran pastor saying that she had gone ahead with her plan. Walter had died and she was hanging onto life at a local hospital. I rushed to the hospital and told the floor nurse that I was her daughter. These were the days before the endless identification needed today was required. I was taken into the critical care unit where Trudy lay sleeping and I whispered to her that I was there. She squeezed my hand in response, woke up, and mumbled to me. After we said the Our Father together, she was smiling. I stayed a while and then told her I'd be back. That evening I got a call that Trudy had died.

At the time this happened, I was completing my thesis for a Master's Degree in Moral Theology at St. Vincent de Paul Seminary. In my classes, we considered all questions surrounding suicide. I had all the book knowledge in the world. I also knew all the philosophical questions around subjectivity. I was upset. I called my friend and theology professor, Father Tom Foudy, and discussed the situation with him. Tom, a bright and wonderful man and superb professor, had a pastoral manner honed from years of integrating teaching with the real life human situations. We concurred. I cannot believe in a God that would do less than take Trudy and Walter in warm loving arms and say: "Welcome, my beloved ones. I have a beautiful place prepared here for you."

The exterior of Manero's (1970) in West Palm Beach with not much growth of the shrubbery.

Searcy Denney Scarola Barnhart & Shipley, P.A.

Our Manero's in West Palm Beach became a favorite place for business people and professionals, so much so that many a day we'd have up to a half-hour wait for lunch. John put together a great luncheon menu, which was popular. One of the partners who worked for a well-known law firm across the street used to be there each day when the door opened to make sure the specials he wanted would not be out by the time the rest of his associates arrived. The firm went through many transitions. Initially we knew them as Montgomery Lytal Reiter Denney & Searcy, P.A. They ate with us almost daily for years and when they split we had to seat the new firm in one room and the old firm in another. Eventually in 1989, the firm, one of the most outstanding in Florida, became Searcy Denney Scarola Barnhart and Shipley, which it is today. Ironically, one of its partners, and our dear friend, Jack Scarola, worked at one of the Manero's Restaurants on Long Island while he was in school, creating in him a lifelong craving for Gorgonzola cheese salad. I remember him teasing John about how one summer, when, after working at the restaurant, he went back to law school while John went on to marry the boss's daughter. In spite of that, our friend Jack married his beautiful wife, Anita, and has done, as the Irish would say in their minimizing way, "not too bad" in the field of law.

Another friend, Emilio Diamantis, a paralegal who has worked at the firm for many years wrote me the following:

> How can I forget John and his unique ways? This is a true story that no one outside Searcy, Denney would know. As you know, we had been eating lunch there forever. John had a set menu each day of the week. Wednesdays was beef tips and they were great. It happened that a certain paralegal had the beef tips one day and lost his job that week. A few months later, it happened again to another person so that no one would order the beef tips any more. That went on for at least two years. One day those of us sitting against the back wall and craving beef tips made a pact: we would all order the tips and see if they would let us all go. When none of us were let go we said the beef tips jinx was broken.

I never knew about the beef tips being jinxed and it didn't seem to reduce sales. Within a few years of opening, we had a thriving lunch business serving anywhere from two hundred fifty to over four hundred in a two-hour stint. We probably knew half of our customers by name and another quarter by face. It was very good, indeed.

The FBI Saves the Day

By the late '70s, we had four beautiful children, with Shannon born in 1973 and Erin in 1977. I remember getting a card on the birth of our last daughter. It read "two and two, lucky you!" Yes, we were the luckiest people in the world with Jay, Rick, Shannon, and Erin adding to our joy. Life was extremely busy.

One busy day I was working on the floor. Our offices were located at the corner of the building. They were "L shaped" so one door went out to the bar and another to the large lobby leading to the dining room. There were three offices with John's in the middle, mine on the lobby end, and the secretary/accountant on the other, near the bar entrance. On this day we had, mistakenly, not locked the accounting door when a young man boldly entered through the accounting side where Joyce, our incredible can-do-anything person, sat. He ran through her office into John's and then through mine, and on his way out picked up my purse. I'm sure the purse was heavy as I had all my "mommy" equipment in it and not much money.

I was taking names at the front hostess stand and saw him running out with my purse and I screamed: "Get him" to anyone in the vicinity. Ironically, waiting in the lobby was an FBI man named Jim O'Brien, a friend and fellow *Cursillo* (a Christian renewal movement which attracted many in our area) participant. Jim was a big guy. He responded immediately and ran out of the lobby, accosted the young kid, and called the police. The thief must have been in shock when someone the size of Jim jumped on him. Who would expect Jim, the FBI person, to be there, hear me scream, and run out the door and send him to the ground with his two hundred fifty pounds of weight? The police came and took the kid to the local station, all for $12.47 in my wallet. The story spread quickly, "Don't mess with those people at Manero's. They have security people all over the place."

The Lord's Place

To the best of my recollection, the Lord's Place (now a thriving community outreach) receptacle was first placed on the premises of Manero's in the late '70s. Back then our friend, Brother Joe Ranieiri, known as Brother Joe (whose brother reportedly died cold and hungry on the streets of New York City), had decided that he wanted to open a food kitchen. This eventually became a homeless shelter and today is an outstanding example of community involvement combining several aspects of outreach such as feeding, clothing, sheltering, and training.

Joe was the catalyst for the Lord's Place in its early years and asked us if he could put the first (clean) garbage dumpster on our property outside our restaurant. I had to talk John into that one, but he agreed. Joe spent three days and three nights living in the dumpster on our property in order to raise awareness and money for the homeless and hungry in the area. As a result, local TV and newspapers began to focus on the plight of the homeless and hungry in Palm Beach County known to be one of the wealthiest areas in the country. We were criticized by some for hosting this on the premises of our well-known restaurant, but most saw it as just what it was: a consciousness-raising plan. That weekend has been repeated in several locations subsequently and today it has grown to an annual Sleep Out with dozens of teams and hundreds of people participating in an overnight on the streets.

Today the Lord's Place is a hugely successful humanitarian operation, not specifically aligned with any church. It is supported by many faiths as well as secular groups in the city of West Palm Beach and in the county. It serves thousands of people with food, shelter, clothing, job skills, and temporary housing for families. It makes me proud to say that, despite criticism, we were there at the Lord's Place's humble beginnings.

Seduced by Gorgonzola

Our families are complete, 1977.
Peter holding January, Bev holding Peter Michael, Dad and Mom, with Rick and Jay in front, me holding Erin, and John holding Shannon.

Bruised but Not Broken

I don't know how many of our employees John bailed out of jail. I believe he thought I was too delicate a person with whom to share that information. He thought I needed to be protected from the harsh realities of life, and at the time, he may have been right. But judging from conversations and letters received after he died, I know it must have been at least a couple of dozen of people he bailed out of trouble. I personally knew of five. John was a master at taking a bruised person and teaching him or her new and better life skills. As long as they were willing to work hard (workaholism being a much valued trait), John had infinite patience with any other of their pecadillos.

Back in the '70s and '80s, all of our job applicants came to us with their records, which they had to obtain from the police and health departments. When the records were no longer required by law, we did background checks on everyone. If they admitted to a small infraction of the law such as problem drinking or marijuana use, John would hire them in an effort to rehabilitate them. We had endless men and some women with these challenges. He taught, mentored, and supported them over the years. Many of them went back to school, got good jobs, married, and had families. He was known in the community to be tough but fair. Rumor had it that one night he was coming home and there was a kids' drinking party in the house across the street from ours. When the kids saw John walking the dog, one yelled out: "Here comes Mr. Mahoney. He's worse than the cops!" This was his reputation but the flipside of that was that you could always call on him at four in the morning. If you were in trouble, he'd be there to help. I'm sure his compassion stemmed from his days in the Navy when more than once he was helped out by a friend or mentor as well.

I always knew these things about John but after he died I received numerous phone calls, letters, and had person-to-person conversations with people who had stories about how he helped them when they were in trouble, temporarily out of a job, or needed just about anything. I used to say that John always had to have a "special person" to help until they got on their feet or sometimes, until they died. When his job was done with one person, he'd find another one immediately. They would just show up at our door, almost knowing that John now had a few free minutes. Perhaps he had these people always on his mind because one day we would go to a funeral and within the next few days, a new person would enter our lives. I admired this greatly and tried to emulate him in my own manner. Our holiday tables were always filled with these people who soon became friends. It was one of the great joys of our life together.

The Social Club

Back in the early '70s when most women with children were still stay-at-home moms, I was invited to join a social club in the area. The group did a lot of good work but I now recognize, unquestionably, it had an air of exclusivity that was less than healthy. To say that the book, *The Help*, was a good representation would be incorrect in my estimation, but there were some similarities. I hear that today these exclusive traits have been tossed aside. Regardless, I made a lot of good friends with great people in this group in the short few years until I resigned.

Seduced by Gorgonzola

Unbeknownst to me, three years into endless meetings and committee gatherings which I attended, John got a call from one of the "lovelies," his affectionate, but somewhat disparaging, name for the members. The social club was publishing a cookbook and wanted our recipe for the Gorgonzola cheese salad dressing. I did not know until after the book was printed that John had refused to give away the recipe. Had the internet been invented back then, all the gals would have had to do would be to look up the recipe as it was to be found in a book entitled, *Nick Manero's Cook-Out Barbecue Book* by Ann Carnahan.[10] This was quite a surprise to me as well as I thought it was only known to a few.

When the club's cookbook was published without the Manero's Gorgonzola recipe, I was flabbergasted and questioned him as to his judgment, especially since most of these gals were our customers and many were friends. I was not happy with his decision. And some of "the lovelies" were not happy with either of us.

Wait for the Dollar Deal

As a result of the empowerment of a beloved and now-deceased priest friend I had taken courses at St. Vincent de Paul Regional Seminary to supplement my psychological training. Courses turned into semesters, which turned into a Master's Degree in Theology in 1989. I worked at the restaurant part time while pursuing my master's degree and raising our family. Life was extremely busy, sometimes dizzying with our children's interests and activities. Both John and I were very involved in our children's schools, our church, and our community.

By 1990, I was still involved in the restaurant but usually in the evenings only, for large parties or special events. I was finally doing the counseling work that I was educated to do and I loved it. I did a lot of volunteer work, mostly at the Cathedral, and with Catholic Charities, the Lord's Place, and the Cursillo Movement.

Within a few years I was able to put my education to work as a pastoral counselor after earning a Doctorate in Ministry in Pastoral Counseling. I loved working in a somewhat normal world (only to find out later that it had its abnormalities and dysfunctions as well). I had become a Vice-President of the National Council of Catholic

Women in Washington and traveled frequently around the country doing leadership training with Catholic women trying to get them to understand that they were not second-class citizens in a man's church.

As previously mentioned, John Mahoney was a giving person who always helped out at local churches, synagogues, and community fundraisers. The restaurant was two blocks from Mary Immaculate Church where I was on staff part time for several years in the '90s. Anyhow, at the local church, we had a senior club that met once a week. John had volunteered to bring a weekly meal, which he would serve to the seniors for five dollars, something which would have cost about eight to ten dollars at local restaurants at the time. John always went out of his way to make this an extraordinary meal and I know that those meals cost us much more than five dollars, not to mention staff costs and his own time. He did this because of who he was: generous and giving to those in need. Regardless of this wonderful deal of a meal, some people would still bring their own meal and we would end up with a few meals left over. After the first week, John decided to sell these leftover meals for one dollar for the church so as not to waste them. He decided this after the first luncheon and it was announced to the group of seniors. The remaining meals were quickly bought up.

When the third week came around, only eighteen of the forty seniors decided to buy the meal. We thought that it was strange to have a drop-off in the lunches after two weeks. John was concerned that they didn't like something that he was preparing. Being a perfectionist with his food, this disturbed him greatly. Having worked with this group for a few years it did not come as a great surprise that after the luncheon when the leftover meals were sold for one dollar, all the meals were quickly grabbed up. Why should they pay five dollars? The other twenty-two people laid in wait for the one-dollar meal to take home for dinner.

Margaret

Margaret was a fanatic churchgoer. And I say this as the daughter of Ellen Manero Tiernan who had few equals among women in the Church unless you counted Joan of Arc or Mother Theresa. Margaret rode her bike each morning to Mary Immaculate Church. On Sundays she attended two churches. First she went to Mary Immaculate and then to Holy Name in time for the eleven o'clock Mass. All of this traveling was by bicycle. It could not have been easy in the ninety-degree heat and Margaret was neither young nor in good health. She was on this path to get all the sanctifying graces and merit she could as she was older and getting ready for finals.

Margaret, we all assumed, was destitute, although she lived in a small apartment in Century Village. She dressed poorly. The people at church tried to help her but she had some obvious emotional problems and was not easy to help. For some reason however, Margaret responded well to John, and as usual, he did what he could to help her. One day he told her to come over after church and he would "provide lunch for her at the restaurant." The following Sunday after her second church appearance on the other side of town, she rode her bike all the way back to Manero's and showed up at the back door asking for John, whose response was to tell her to come to the front door like everyone else, not the back door.

That was the beginning. From that day forward, Margaret came almost daily to the restaurant where she was seated and provided with a lovely lunch or dinner. John instructed all our coworkers to take good care of her and to give him the check. He would take care of their tip. She ate like a queen each day and then got on her bike and drove home. After about two months, Margaret stopped coming. Everyone wondered what happened to her. We checked with her neighbors at Century Village. She hadn't been to church and no one had seen her. We became worried. Finally, the local pastor even had her apartment checked to make sure she wasn't dead. We thought perhaps she had been hit on her bike and lay in a ditch somewhere. She was accustomed to being on the streets, but this was just too long. The mystery lasted for about four weeks.

We were all shocked when Margaret returned to both church and Manero's. She was treated with a hero's welcome and all were happy to see her in one piece. Whatever had happened to her, we were glad she survived her ordeal. Actually, she looked a little better than usual. She looked more tan, so we thought maybe a relative had cared for her for a while. When questioned on her whereabouts Margaret said that she had decided to take a trip to Europe. Margaret, the traveler, had decided to take a trip all over Europe by Euro train. She had toured seven countries in three weeks. To say that we were all flabbergasted would be an understatement.

I can still see blessed Margaret today as she has peddled her way into the Great Heavenly banquet in the sky.

Surveillance on the Roof

One of the great, and not so great, realities of the restaurant business is that you never know what you'll be doing next. This is usually exacerbated by the fact that restaurants are known for attracting both the best and the worst of humanity, in terms of coworkers. Many young people, thinking they have invented the newest ways of cheating their employer out of a few bucks, a few steaks or a few cases of beer, would be surprised to know that their plots are not unique, surprising, or even new.

Back in the early '90s we had a severe problem of losing steaks and filets, both of which came with a substantial cost. Losing a box or two once in a while was one thing but we were losing a box or two a week and could not figure it out. We were assisted in this dilemma by Allen, one of our managers who loved to do what he called "perimeter patrol." Both John and I knew that meant that he needed to get out of the constant stress for a few minutes and get a few breaths of air while walking around the restaurant. It was probably better for his productivity anyway so we just went along with him and considered this part of his duties. We never had really done "perimeter patrol" before Allen. He had been in the Coast Guard and I wouldn't be surprised if that is where he got the idea.

Allen was a wonderful young man who volunteered to do a stakeout on the roof in an effort to get to the root of the lost steak situation. We had about ten to fourteen people working in the kitchen on any given night. So without any other employees knowing it, Allen climbed up on the roof with a flashlight one summer's night about eight thirty and intended to stay there until closing, the time during which we felt the pilferage was taking place. After three long hours on the roof we still had no results.

The second night...same thing. But Allen was not to be deterred. "Stay calm; maintain" was his motto. Eventually he would get his man.

On the third night however, the stage was about to have actors. Allen arrived with his pitcher of iced tea to keep himself awake. He also was prepared with spyglasses, flashlights, and a camera. He watched as one of our young chefs walked out the back door with bags of garbage which he laid down on the ground next to a filled garbage dumpster. We didn't know until later that he had marked the garbage bag filled with the NY sirloin steaks with an old kitchen cloth. All the bags were left for about ten minutes. When no one was around, a woman came along, picked up the bag with the old cloth wrapped around it and put it in her car. As this was before cell phones, texting and such, the timing was remarkable.

Allen clicked pictures of the girl, got them developed at a one-hour photo, and the next day the s--- hit the fan as John Mahoney, "worse than the cops," questioned the young chef and soon after, fired him. John was happy. Allen was elated and from that time forward not only did we not scoff at "perimeter patrol" but it became part of the protocol at Manero's.

Martha's Kitchen

For all those people who think running a restaurant is a dream, I invite you to heed the words of our beloved friend, Martha Heimbach, who ran a small breakfast and luncheon spot for us for a few years in downtown West Palm Beach. These words below, written by Martha, an RN by profession, and an exceptionally organized person, are sure to dissuade anyone who has delusions of restaurant management grandeur:

> It seemed like a great idea. One night visiting John and Donna Mahoney, after several glasses of wine, we discussed the small café Manero's had opened in downtown West Palm Beach. The café, then called Good News, had lost the manager that John had opened

the café to employ. The small café was on the first floor of a very old hotel across the street from the courthouse. At this time there were no restaurant facilities in the courthouse and few eating establishments in the downtown area. Since the café was a few blocks from the school that our children attended, I decided that this would be a perfect fit for my love of cooking and entertaining. I would drive the carpool to St. Ann School and then open the café, now renamed Martha's Kitchen, to serve breakfast and lunch. There was already a loyal established clientele of attorneys and judges eating there regularly.

I immediately found two assistants to help me with this endeavor, my eighty-year-old father-in-law, George, and a friend, Laverne. Manero's supplied us with the soup of the day and fresh cut meats for sandwiches. I baked homemade cookies and cakes at home to serve as desserts. Martha's Kitchen opened and was immediately met with great enthusiasm from the downtown employees. The customers that we didn't plan for were the inhabitants of the old hotel. A number of those residents had substance abuse addictions or other mental disabilities and frequently yelled obscenities at customers or engaged in rowdy arguments. We had our work cut out for us.

The most profit came from take-outs. Many days we would receive large orders for sequestered juries. This required a lot of teamwork and more help than we had at the time. So John sent me *Dave* who was a high school drop-out John was trying to rehabilitate. John took him under his wing and taught him some basic skills. As long as John was watching him all was well. When John thought Dave was ready to have a looser leash he sent him to us. The poor guy had no teeth so we had to keep him out of the sight of customers. He would help out in back while we were serving lunch but everything he cooked he burned.

One day I went to the kitchen and no Dave. In a panic, I ran outside and found Dave feeding our roast beef to four or five of his buddies who were shooting up at the back door. I called John immediately and he called the police who came and took them all, including my sous chef, off to the local booking department in handcuffs. It was then that John came down and for a few days took over as cook. But John couldn't stay for long as he had a larger restaurant to run.

We then found Joan and *Will*. Joan was very capable so I went back to the kitchen. She was a friend who would work as a waitress. Will lived in the hotel and claimed to be a first-class chef. The problem with Will was that he wanted to garnish everything including a hardboiled egg. Will's employment ended after several weeks when he arrived in the morning under the influence and very agitated. When he threatened me with his chef's knife, I backed out of the kitchen and quietly called John for assistance. John arrived within minutes, hauled inebriated Will into the back alley, and as he would phrase it, "cleaned his clock." We never saw Will again.

The eating habits of many of the regular customers were a bit on the strange side. One prominent judge would be the first morning customer. His standing order for breakfast was black coffee and burnt toast. He sent the toast back many times because it wasn't charred enough. (His mother must have been a great cook.) One morning, he arrived early as we were opening. At the same time, out of the corner of my eye, I could see a large rodent stuck in a glue trap that the exterminator had attached to a ceiling pipe. The poor fellow was not dead and he was trying to free himself. My assistant calmly picked up a broom and clobbered him to death, having him fall to the floor in front of us. She then lovingly picked him up asking God to forgive her for killing one of his beautiful creatures. I guess the judge never saw this or didn't care because he kept coming back for his burnt toast.

Every morning my darling 85-year-old father-in-law would drive from Boynton Beach to assist me. His job was cashier. We did not have a cash register or calculator so Dad would sit at the door with pencil and pad in hand asking each person what they had for lunch. Within seconds he would total the bill and add "Uncle Sam's six percent."

I learned so many lessons in the year that I was a Manero's employee; the main one being that it is not as easy as most people think to operate any kind of eating establishment. I thank my dear friends, Donna and John, for allowing me the opportunity to cross that off my bucket list.

Our friend, Martha, returned to work with her husband, George, who was a well-known obstetrician/gynecologist in West Palm Beach. He was delighted to have her back in his office and she certainly recognized that it was easier dealing with the ever-changing and volatile hormones of pregnant women than dealing with the patrons and coworkers at Martha's Kitchen.

Seduced by Gorgonzola

Martha Heimbach and me, years later.
One of the greatest blessings of my life!

The Bar at Manero's

On any given afternoon at Manero's in West Palm Beach, Carlos stationed himself in the center of the bar. John and I met Carlos, who was from Barcelona, on a cruise we had taken to the Caribbean in the early '70s. Over the long weekend, we came to know and like him. At the end of the cruise, John left Carlos his business card, in case Carlos wanted a job in the States. It was only a few weeks before Carlos did call and we began the long and drawn-out process of sponsoring him for citizenship.

It was one of the best things we ever did as Carlos was a class act. He was loyal, honest, interested, and interesting. On top of all that, he conducted the bar like a well-integrated orchestra. He knew just when to move to or from a patron. He also had the gift of pouring oil on troubled waters and could calm most any disturbance without calling for John. He had great people skills and it was a sad day when he had to leave. He worked with us for several years until his wife's parents needed more care and Carlos and his wife moved to Miami to help them. We were saddened by this loss for with Carlos at the bar, we felt it was in good hands.

Seated around the bar might be a young couple, Maggie and John, with whom we formed a lifelong friendship. He was from Pratt Whitney and she worked for a local gynecologist. They would come in about once a week and he always wanted liver and onions, one of our specialties. Maggie, meanwhile, came for the "mouth-watering prime rib" and an occasional Grey Goose. Next to them would be a circuit court judge who would come in about three times a week. He was a well-respected gentleman who would often come in with associates. His case load, apparently, was overwhelming and he sought comfort in Jack Daniels.

Also at the bar would be *Jack G.*, a local golf professional, who started each evening with us before moving to more serious clubs where he could "pick up chicks." Jack came in every day for about four years until we never saw or heard from him again. Rumor had it that one of these "chicks" had reformed him. Close by there were two gay men, who drove miles to come to our bar as they did not want to be recognized in their respective work areas. They lived together far away from where each of them worked. One was a realtor and another was a physician's assistant. They were super nice and both were still in the closet. But then, this was many years ago.

A beloved friend, Tom, along with some surgical sales representatives, would sit in the booth nearest the door. I can always remember the way he took his keys out of his pocket and intentionally put them down on the table as if to say: "The day is over, now time to enjoy!" Then there would be *Don and Jan* who owned a travel agency. They came in religiously when Carlos was there and never when he wasn't scheduled as they did not care for "your other bartender."

A frequent visitor, who always surprised us, was *Pat*, a local contractor who was a Jehovah's Witness and was constantly leaving the *Watchtower* with other patrons as well as with John. As many times as John told him he was secure in his faith and not concerned about going

Seduced by Gorgonzola

to hell because he was Catholic, Pat persisted. Often we would find *Watchtowers* under the office door or in the men's room. Regardless, he always downed two scotch and waters before proceeding to look for his next potential conversion.

If it were March or early April, you could find Bobby Cox, then manager of the Atlanta Braves, along with Billy Acree, and Pete Skorput, the spring training director, Phil Niekro, and several members of the Braves. They came in frequently, adding great interest as they were friendly and outgoing with other guests. We did all the special parties for the Braves at the local stadium where they had their spring training before moving to Orlando. Often Ted Turner and Jane Fonda would attend these events as well. My sons, Jay and Rick, have great memories of these events and super stories ready for another book. They were frequently bat boys for them and to this day they never fail to go to at least one game a season in Atlanta.

One of the fellows who worked for us, Richard Rainey, offered this delightful story:

> ...Another time, Phil Niekro, pitcher for the Atlanta Braves, got his Lincoln Continental stuck under the porté-cochere, at 7:00 p.m. on a Saturday night. Back in those days the Lincolns would automatically lock themselves once you exited the vehicle. Some digital buttons on the driver side door would reopen once you punched in the right numbers. Problem was Niekro was not driving. Apparently, he had loaned it to an acquaintance of his. No one knew the combination to get back into this running vehicle, holding up traffic and stinking up the place with exhaust fumes. John showed up, obviously from home, and was absolutely livid pointing the finger at one of our crew (who had wrecked another vehicle two weeks before) asking: "Did you do this?" It took forever to get that car moved because the driver had to find Niekro wherever he was and get the passkey to get back into the car. I remember Jules and

Charlie (hosts) were out there having us type in Niekro's jersey number, Braves, etc. It was totally hilarious later but not at that time. It took about forty-five minutes to finally get it moved after they found Niekro.

Our restaurant stories are endless. Some can be printed; others cannot. In addition to these we had so many regulars, who just came in every day as part of their routine. Looking back, in addition to great food and service, I think many of our guests were seeking acceptance and companionship and for some, something to take away the loneliness which is part of all of our lives. Each of them had their own story and each of them taught us lessons that we needed to learn and perhaps have integrated into our lives.

The Party of Parties

In the spring of 1998, John was in remission from a stage four cancer diagnosis which he had received on March 28 of 1997. I shall never forget the terror of that day, a Good Friday, which has had multiple meanings for me ever since. The community, headed by a few great friends, knew that John had been challenged by colon cancer and that we were also moving our business of twenty-eight years to another town thirty miles away. Most of them couldn't believe it but it was a decision that John and I had made after realizing that the area where we had our business had greatly changed. Crime was becoming a problem for us. Cars were broken into on a frequent basis and our staff and guests' safety was a big concern.

As a result of these events, many friends complemented by many of our purveyors, planned a huge party at a local country club and invited community leaders, personal and business friends, and a variety of people who had come to admire John over the years. It was the kind of honor that everyone would be proud of but few are blessed to experience. It was a true outpouring of love, admiration, and affection unparalleled in most lifetimes.

All the members of our family came home from wherever they were. My parents drove from North Carolina, Jay from Jacksonville where he was working for Marriott, Rick from our business, J. Arthur's in North Carolina, Erin from college in North Carolina, and Shannon from her law school studies. In addition, about four hundred people came from the community to honor John and by extension, me.

A limo was sent to pick up the entire family and when we arrived at our destination, a spectacular new country club in the area, a roomful of hundreds of people burst into applause. It was beyond our belief; friends came from all over the country to be at this extraordinary party honoring John. There were wonderful surprises lurking in every corner and we were most touched by friends who had long since moved away who had returned for this event. Even many from the Braves, including Bobby Cox, the manager of the team, were there. It was exciting, nerve-racking, and a happy and sad occasion — all at once, a once-in-a-lifetime experience for mere mortals. Metallic balloons with our pictures on them were flying all over the ballroom. The highlight of the evening was a twenty-minute video in which our twenty-eight years and various events were honored in a humorous and delightful way. My favorite was a scene in which they copied our well-known outdoor chef's hat sign that has always read: "Always bring the children." They had removed those words and replaced them with: "Leave the little bastards at home!"

There were speeches by all, commendations in word and in print from local and state officials as well as the local bishop, and then finally a few words from us. Even some of our kids spoke and shared the many times that John had "fired" them from our family business. We laughed and we cried. We thanked the community profusely and I invited them to join us for Gorgonzola cheese salad and wine at Christmas in our new venture in Palm City. It was a night of incredible meaning, joy, and profound sadness all rolled into one.

Many of those people did join us in Palm City.

John was not to be among us.

Customer Letter

Dear Donna,

Sending loving memories of Manero's and J. Arthur's. Watched both being built. A charter dining/member of 2200 Palm Beach Lakes Boulevard. You, John, and family/staff, produced wonderful memories for our family. Many "Soul Prints." Quite sure that the obvious reasons for the success of Manero's and J. Arthur's have been covered at this point. Your endearing giving back to your patrons should be noted.

Manero's became a magnet...those that were fortunate to enter your doors, were drawn back again and again.

My children still speak of our special dinner times together at Manero's — two to three times weekly and always birthdays, with their name on the illuminated billboard, something they, as well as, yours truly, will always remember. Manero's...Always Bring the Children.

I miss John, and thank him for his unselfish work ethic, and helping those that needed it the most. Blessings to you and all of your family. You and they, carry forward. Manero's/J. Arthur's.

Tom

The Wrecking Ball

One of the saddest days of John's and my life was the demolition of Manero's in West Palm Beach in July of 1998. After long discussion in late 1996, we decided to sell the property where we had started our business. We had decided to move our business north as the area was changing. We had considered moving downtown but were not convinced that the downtown West Palm Beach area was ready yet for our restaurant. In the end, the decision was made to move about a half-hour north to an up-and-coming community in Martin County called Palm City.

As a result of John's devastating diagnosis however, we considered backing out of the life-changing decision we had made to relocate our business. But upon reflection, we mutually decided that this was his dream and so it should have positive effects on his dismal diagnosis. By the time the restaurant actually closed, John was one year and five months into treatment. It was only a few days later that the wrecking crew came in and literally crashed into our twenty-eight years of history, leaving as the only visible signs nothing but rubble. It was traumatic.

A month later on August 8, 1998, John died. Looking back, the wrecking ball became a metaphor for the cancer and treatment, which wracked his body until there was nothing left. A wrecking ball remains one of the saddest symbols of my life. Today a Walgreens stands where once thousands of people met, shared meals, made relationships, celebrated birthdays, anniversaries, life and death, got on their knees and proposed to their beloved, and entered into contracts which would bind them for decades. Weekly when I'm in the area, many people still say to me: "Every time I go by Walgreens, I still can't believe that Manero's is gone."

Nor can I.

Life is either a daring adventure or nothing.
—Helen Keller

CHAPTER 4

J. Arthur's in Maggie Valley, North Carolina

The Purchase of the Property

You never know who will change the entire direction of your life. Looking back, one of the craziest, least thought through, unbusinesslike, and unplanned things we have ever done was to buy the property for the restaurant in Maggie Valley, North Carolina. It was also one of the best decisions that we ever made.

The year was 1984 and my parents both had retired. They bought a home in North Carolina in 1978 as a result of a connection with a Hallandale customer, Ruth Martin, who was a local realtor in Waynesville. She and her husband, Ted, were well known in the little town and owned Martin's Electric on Main Street there. Waynesville is the next town over from Maggie Valley, in the Smoky Mountains of western North Carolina. The Martins would visit South Florida each year with their son, Scotty, and spend many evenings at Manero's.

When my parents retired, Ruth, then a realtor, encouraged them to make a trip to Waynesville. She showed Mom and Dad a lovely home with an exquisite mountain view, in a secluded area of the town. They fell in love with the home and bought it. John and I and my brother, Peter, and sister-in law, Bev, and our families spent as much time there as possible during the summers and holidays. We also brought many of our friends from South Florida who were all happily and graciously hosted by my parents.

Soon after moving into their mountain home, Mom and Dad decided to do some remodeling. The gentleman doing the work on their property was Roger McElroy. Roger was married with three teenage children, one of whom would follow him on his jobs. Within a few years my parents became close friends with the builder and his family and especially his middle son, Herb, who had just lost his grandfather and who had adopted my dad as his "new grandfather." Roger and his wife, Donna, lived in the middle of Maggie Valley with Donna's mother, an older and very bright woman, also a realtor. Her name was Irene Julien.

In late 1983 we came up to North Carolina after Christmas with our four kids, hoping to see a little snow and do a little skiing at Cataloochee and to spend time with Mom and Dad. We had been having a wonderful time in the cold and snow and all the kids were in their glory. The vacation had been both relaxing, as well as energizing. On New Year's Day, we were all invited to a house party at the McElroys' home. The McElroys frequently had wonderful parties at their home, which at that time was on the property of their motel, the Meadowlark. On this particular afternoon they told Mom and Dad specifically to bring all the kids and grandkids — their parties were multigenerational and our four rambunctious kids were welcome to play pool, ping pong, and other games throughout the large, rambling house.

The New Year's Day party began in the late afternoon and we arrived about four o'clock. By around five o'clock, we had become comfortable with the McElroys, Donna's mother, Irene Julien, and their three kids, Joe, Herb, and Cindy along with all their extended family and friends. They were the kind of people who just made you feel at home. John, no longer a drinker, had struck up a lively conversation with Ms. Julien and I joined in.

Out of the blue, or so it seemed, Ms. Julien said to us: "How about us taking a ride around? There are a few places I'd like to show you." Our four kids were running around the house like wild cats, being encouraged in that by the older McElroy kids. I said to Ms. Julien that we could never leave the kids, but we were assured that all would be well and were encouraged to go with Irene. It was already dark out and I couldn't imagine what this smart (but somewhat kooky, I was then thinking) woman had in store. We drove around in her large white car to see four open properties. I could not comprehend the reason at the time. Within thirty minutes she had us interested in building a restaurant on one of those four properties. This was nothing short of crazy. After all, we resided 720 miles away, had four young children and a thriving and totally consuming business. How could we possibly think of a restaurant that far away? And why would we want to?

I'm not sure if it was inspiration or insanity, but by the next morning we had pretty well decided that we would buy the property across from the Meadowlark Motel. We consulted with my parents who said they would help financially. (Many years later after Dad's death, it occurred to me that he probably set this whole thing up once again.) So late on the morning of January 2 we signed a contract on the property at 2843 Soco Road in Maggie Valley that would, within a few years, be known as J. Arthur's Restaurant. We chose this name to honor my dad, who for years had operated everything he owned in the name of the Manero family.

It was one of the quickest, quirkiest, craziest, most thoughtless, "no business plan" decisions we ever made. At the same time it was divinely inspired and quintessentially brilliant. It would be the place for a lifetime of memories as John and I raised our kids in dual residences. Thank God for Ms. Julien, a visionary angel, who came out of nowhere to alter the course of our lives for all time.

Dad and me at the beginning of construction of
J. Arthur's in Maggie Valley, 1985.

The Restaurant

The building in Maggie Valley was and is beautiful. It sits in the middle of town, a two-story A-frame seating about 220 people in its entirety. The downstairs has a large dining room with a bar on the other side of the main floor. The bar has ten booths and counter seating, comfortably accommodating about fifty guests. The dining room, which seats about a hundred people, is comfortable and upbeat. Upstairs there is a small private room that can seat parties of twenty-five and a large open space, which seats another fifty-five. The kitchen is in the back of the restaurant. The structure was constructed by our family friend, Roger McElroy, a superb builder and later, mayor of Maggie Valley. The architect was Richard San Giovanni who worked with John and me to give us exactly what we had planned. Dick was a friend of ours from Florida and was well known for many of the spectacular churches in Florida. He also did our remodeling in West Palm Beach after a fire. Dick was a master and both he and Roger did an extraordinary job of which we have always been very proud.

When we opened in August 1986, we weren't quite sure how we would handle it. We were determined to stay there for the summer. After that each of us would take four or five days usually once a month and travel north. Sometimes we flew but mostly we traveled by car. John went most of the time as I was taking care of the children but about one out of every four or five times I would head north to handle whatever business was necessary to be checked. We had a superb staff at the time so after we got things organized and running, the system worked quite well for many years. In the beginning, we closed in the winter months because it was just too difficult for us to handle with our business in Florida. Moreover, it was not profitable to run the restaurant in the winter. Within a few years, we realized that this situation would be impossible for our employees if they were to have stable economic lives so we decided to bite the bullet and stay open during the winter months at least four to five days a week. We have always incurred a loss during the winter season but it has been worth it to maintain a stable and good staff.

Maggie Valley is a beautiful and unique little community. The people in Maggie Valley are beyond friendly. I always used to say that there was something that happened when people stepped over the North Carolina line. That was the time when their frowns became smiles. The same people who would run you over in Florida were all of a sudden stopping to say hello. The business people here, many original Floridians, make a great effort to help each other and it would not be unusual to share employees or borrow when we run out of supplies. Joey's Pancake House, a longtime success story with its owner and our dear friend, Brenda O'Keefe, has helped us out in many situations. We try to reciprocate. A wonderful irony of life is that my friends, Rich and Sue Gays' daughter and son-in-law, Debbie and Louis Perrone, opened a restaurant near us a few years ago, Frankie's Trattoria, which serves the best Italian food around. There are many wonderful and dedicated businesses in Maggie that make it a great place to live and work. Our big attractions have been Wheels through Time Motorcycle Museum, Ghost Town in the Sky, and of course, the Cataloochee Ski Area in the winter. The natural beauty of the area is phenomenal, and hiking, fishing, biking, and many other outdoor activities attract visitors. The leaf-changing season is our favorite and people come from all over to see what Mother Nature has done. The Chamber of Commerce is staffed with talented people of good will who are willing to work hard to achieve success. Over the years, Maggie Valley has had its up-and-downs and has created a lot of interest for both locals and tourists. It has been good for us and we hope that we have been good for it. When my parents were alive, the restaurant was a real source of joy for them and they ate there almost every night when they were in town. Dad was so proud to have a restaurant in his name.

The menu at J. Arthur's is similar to the menu of our other restaurants, slightly more geared to mountain fare but primarily focused on great prime rib, steaks, fish, Gorgonzola cheese salad, home-made soups and a variety of other menu selections necessary to run a profitable restaurant today. In the last several years, the farm-to-table movement has become popular across the country. The Food Revolution has spread all over the country and western North Carolina has not been excluded from this shift, as the predominance of television shows featuring farm fresh has made a big impact on all. We try to buy as much food and as many local products as possible to support the local economy. This, of course, depends on the time of the year and the category of food, as some foods are impossible or too expensive to buy locally. In addition we have nightly specials often geared to the particular time of the year or special groups who visit the area.

All in all, it was one of the best decisions we ever made.

J. Arthur's in Maggie Valley.

The Septic Tank in Maggie Valley

When we first opened our new restaurant, there were more than a few challenges, but none more exasperating than the septic tank. Maggie Valley, at the time, had no sewers, so both John and I met with the town manager and the water plant manager about this situation and what effect a large restaurant like ours would have on the Valley. We were required to put in a septic tank, which we operated for close to three years until sewers came to town. The septic tank became the bane of our existence as every afternoon and evening one of us (almost always John, sometimes with Rick or Jay) would have to go out to the west side of the restaurant and stir the tank in an effort to keep it all functioning and keep the neighbors from complaining about the unpleasant odors.

When the wind was blowing in a westerly direction, we would frequently get complaints from an adjacent motorhome park about the oppressive smell. We would pray for the wind to blow in any direction but from the east. What were we supposed to do as we certainly understood their complaints but were confined by Mother Nature's whims and winds? It was an unpleasant situation and along with many other challenges of starting a restaurant in a tourist town, was the last thing we needed. Thank God, after two summers we were able to hook up to sewers. We could not have been happier if we had won the lottery. These are the kind of things you try to forget…or…on a tough day, you remember and smile, knowing you will survive whatever the current challenge.

Astonished!

For the opening of the restaurant I wanted the ladies restroom to be extremely beautiful so I carefully did all the last-minute appointments myself: pictures, flower vases filled with fresh stunning colors, and small feminine decor. I did this with absolute certainty that after the opening week all of these things would be missing. I didn't care because I wanted it perfect for our debut. In our Florida restaurant we had to screw everything to the walls; even two-by-three foot pictures, either in the lobby or in the bars. Everything had to be bolted in West Palm Beach because somehow things would mysteriously disappear. In Florida, it was not unusual for salt and pepper shakers, bread baskets, specialty martini glasses, and dinnerware to disappear in no time. I'm convinced that in more than one house in South Florida you may attend a sizeable barbecue and enjoy your meals while cutting your beef with several sets of misappropriated Manero's steak knives.

Suffice it to say that I was shocked to open our business in Maggie Valley (a God-fearing, churchgoing, gun slinging area of the country) to find that it took almost three years before one of my pieces of art in the ladies room went missing. I just could not believe that not one thing was taken in all that time. I would check repeatedly to reinforce my incredulity. When finally something disappeared all I could think to myself was that it was probably someone from South Florida who hauled off the goods.

John and me in front of J. Arthur's in Maggie Valley.

The Fish Run

Looking back over our twenty-nine years in Maggie Valley I think of the many things we have done to keep the restaurant viable. The season is basically four months plus the Christmas holidays. Anything over that is bonus. Many adjustments out of the ordinary business cycle have to be made. In addition, owners have to do every job from the most menial to the most exciting to keep the flow and the business successful.

A couple of months ago, my husband, Tim, and I went to a Sysco restaurant show in Knoxville, Tennessee. As we were crossing the mountains over I-40 from North Carolina to Tennessee, I was thinking back a quarter of a century to the times when I would do what I affectionately called the "fish run," which required about five hours to get one hundred pounds of fish that was shipped from South Florida. It was a two-hour ride to the commercial airport in Knoxville, an hour or so to procure the package, and a two-hour ride back home, sometimes in driving rain or terrible traffic, on the curvy and mountainous I-40.

Today we get our fresh fish delivered, but years ago we could not find fresh fish anywhere in the western part of North Carolina. Trout, of course, was plentiful from the many wonderful local trout farms, but that was the extent of the fresh fish to be found. Since we always preferred to serve, and guests preferred to order fresh fish, it was critical to make the fish run at least twice a week. Sometimes I made the trip with one or more of our four kids in the backseat. Those were the days before car seats or even seat belts. Those were also the days before the iPod, the iPad, the iPhone, or many of the other "I" devices that keep kids occupied. Even the Gameboy did not exist back then, so additionally, I had to keep them entertained as well. Those really were ancient times.

My memories of the fish run remind me of those many things John and our family did to make J. Arthur's a success and the many challenges we have had: the two successive Fourth of Julys during which the electricity (meaning air conditioning as well as the ability to operate) went out right at six in the evening; our delivery truck, which was stolen the night before a huge catering event; the accident right in front of the restaurant which closed us down on the Sunday before Labor Day (one of our busiest days) as the road in front of the restaurant became a helicopter pad; the fire in the laundry room when everyone, except for me, was out of town; the time we ran out of our famous prime rib at seven in the evening with about two hundred guests still waiting to be served, and the time that almost all of our employees had the flu and we had to borrow employees from Joey's Pancake House. Having options and being flexible is critical in our business and the old Girl Scout motto to always "be prepared" has many times been put to the test.

Mom and Dad, circa 1987.

Mom

When Ellen Tiernan was alive, it was important for her to be involved in the family business however she could. In earlier times she would work nights as a hostess/cashier and entertain customers as well. As she got into her later '70s and early '80s she still wanted to participate, but could not work nights any longer. It was then that she decided that she would become the laundry lady.

Each morning (except Sunday) usually after her exercise class, Mom would drive from her mountain home in Waynesville to the restaurant. She would then begin the vigorous task of sorting, washing, drying, folding, and stacking all the laundry — these were the days of white tablecloths and napkins and there were always piles. After she would clean everything, she would completely set the tables, with linens, glassware, and silver for the evening meal. This happened until the health department came in and proclaimed that the silver and glassware could not be put out until just before opening.

We paid her for this work and once a month she would take the entire amount and divide it between a dozen or more of her charities. I remember many March mornings over the years, going to the tax accountant with Dad who probably had two hundred or more checks made out to mostly Catholic organizations for their charitable deductions. Many times he implored me to have her do this once a year, so as to have less paperwork, but she would not be moved.

I shall never forget one morning when she entered the restaurant in a rush. Usually she changed her clothes at the gym, but this morning she had planned to change at the restaurant. Since the restaurant is right on the highway, people buzzed by in droves every morning between eight and nine o'clock. Whatever happened on the restaurant property was quite visible to the community. Now remember, back then, things were different. People did not run around town in their gym clothes as they do now. And remember, too, I was quite different, trying to live up to the standards taught me by the Madams of the Sacred Heart at Manhattanville. You did not run around town in gym clothes, especially if you had shrunk from five foot two inches to four foot ten inches and your weight had compressed itself as you shrunk.

Anyhow, this morning I happened to look out the window of the summer home next to the restaurant and I saw Mom get out of her car in a skintight leotard, with all of her one hundred and sixty pounds, somewhat like a butterball, squeezed into her four foot ten frame. It was not her best look. I looked at John in a panic and immediately ran to the front door and grabbed a trench coat and tried to put it on her, admonishing her for appearing in public in the inappropriate outfit. She, Ellen Tiernan, the original church lady, looked angrily at me and said to me: "Donna, you are such a tightass! I can do anything that I want to do!" She then proceeded into the restaurant, changed into her work clothes, and began her day. It was the last time I critiqued her outerwear.

Over the years, I have thought of that story and Mom's participation numerous times and I realize that my mom taught me many lessons:

1. Everyone needs to be valued for whatever way they participate. So many times when I witness the shoddy work done by people

today, I would so welcome (and so miss) Mom's participation in the restaurant.
2. No job is beneath one's dignity. Everyone needs to feel like they are contributing in some way, and this does not change as we age. Mom's morning job was never beneath her dignity and it gave meaning to her days.
3. Lighten up, Donna. Just see the joy and humor in each situation rather than critiquing.
4. Keep her words in mind in case I will soon be needing them with my own children.

The Indomitable Lee Parker

Words escape me for the quintessential woman who was Lee Parker. One of a kind, elegant, bright, fun, frisky, generous, friendly, and always, a mystery. She would love that I am writing this about her. Our family first met Lee when she came to dine at J. Arthur's in the late '80s. Who could miss her? Even at her age, whatever it was, all eyes would turn when Lee entered the room. She stood out in a crowd, especially in Maggie Valley. Our town is a tourist town. When you come to eat you can dress up or dress down. Dressing down would mean t-shirt, jeans, and old sneakers or boots. Dressing up would be a nice t-shirt, clean jeans, and maybe real shoes. Anything more is overdressed. Wearing your tropical clothes is out of place, wearing a dress is for church only, and wearing Palm Beach classics is absolutely taboo.

The first time and many other times Lee walked into J. Arthur's she was with her entourage. She never dressed down in anything less than haute couture clothing. These were dresses with sparkles and glitter, high heels, and often, a wide-brimmed hat. Lee wore large dark glasses, reminiscent of a Hollywood star of the 1960s. She spoke softly. I can't imagine any server going to her table and saying: "Hey, guys, how are you tonight?" Even the most poorly trained server would have to intuitively know this. After all…you were serving Lee Parker.

In spite of all the above, Lee Parker was as common as the girl next-door: warm, loving, compassionate, and always looking out for the underdog. She had been in the Rockettes and then worked for Ma

Bell for many years. She had to struggle quite a bit herself, although, through an accident of fate, she became the caretaker for a wealthy man who left her as trustee for his massive fortune. She was able to live very well off the fund and able to be generous to her family, friends, and her favorite charities as she knew that when she died everything that was left was to go to the gentleman's alma mater.

When Lee came into J. Arthur's, she would request a different server each time, as she wanted everyone to have a chance to serve her table and to "take care of them," meaning she would leave them a fifty-dollar tip, no matter how small the check. She became close to our whole family and we were invited to all her parties whether in Maggie Valley or in South Florida. One evening she invited me for a girls night out for just the two of us in Asheville. She had asked me to drive her Cadillac as her night vision was not great, and I agreed. We went to a lovely French restaurant where everyone knew her.

On the way over, she said she was going to take me into her confidence and tell me her real age, which she had not told anyone. I was honored. To me, she seemed ageless. She told me she was sixty-five and I reacted in shock. It wasn't that I didn't believe her but that she actually would share this information with me was a surprise. After all, she was a diva. To me at forty, she could have been fifty-five. All I knew was that she was older and a little eccentric, but just a little. Mostly she was just fun. She was delighted that I was shocked, although at the time I didn't exactly comprehend why.

Seduced by Gorgonzola

Jay, Shannon, Erin, and Rick with the indomitable, Lee Parker. Grandma Maria Grace's picture over Lee's head.

We would see Lee often in the mountains every summer for years and occasionally in South Florida when she would host big events. She was kind to our kids and we invited her to our place in West Palm Beach frequently, especially to family gatherings on holidays. The years passed, and by my calculations, Lee must have been about seventy-two judging from the night she told me she was sixty-five. Out of the blue one week, we received two birthday invitations for parties for Lee. When the first one showed up we were delighted. When the second one showed up it said that we were cordially invited to celebrate "Lee Parker's 90th birthday party." Ninety? By my calculations she was in her early seventies. That meant that when she took me into "her confidence" and told me she was sixty-five, she was actually eighty-two. That little stinker. Was I the only one she fooled that way?

As the summer went on, we realized that Lee wanted as many birthday parties as possible. Parties were her "raison d'être." John and I got on the bandwagon and gave her one on our patio. We brought in a country band and hosted about sixty of her closest friends. She had, as mentioned, been in the Rockettes and she spent the night kicking up her high heels, sometimes as high as two feet in the air. I kept thinking "God, please don't let her fall." But despite my concerns and the few glasses of wine Lee consumed, she did not fall and she did not stop dancing in her beads and bangles all night long. She fully enjoyed herself. At one stage during the night, a priest friend gave her an Irish blessing, "Slainte agus go merried beo ar an sho aris," which he translated to mean: "To your good health and may you be alive and kicking and making love again this time next year." Lee, who believed in making hay while the sun was still shining, looked him straight in the eye and said slowly, unabashedly and seductively, "Father, why wait until next year?"

(This was the last party that we would host together in Maggie Valley, as unknown to us then, John would soon be diagnosed with his illness.)

Mother of the Bride

In the restaurant business, we see it all. I have come not to be surprised by anything. The mother of the bride was certainly not the worst, but she did provide us a few chuckles. Several years back, we had a woman looking for a place for a wedding party of fifty. We told her we could easily accommodate her in our upstairs party space and that we had served many wedding parties over the years. She wanted soup to nuts, an intimate but elegant wedding, but there was to be no alcohol. She just did not want people drinking and spoiling the moment for her daughter. With the advice of St. Paul in mind that "a little wine is good for the stomach," I always encourage hosts and hostesses to provide at least one glass during the welcoming. But "mother of the bride" was adamant. We met with her and promised to provide her with everything just the way she dictated.

On the day of the party, the reception had begun and all was going well. The guests had their appetizers and punch and were about to sit for their main course when I realized that I needed a clarification from the bride's mother so I went upstairs to find her. She was nowhere to be found among the happy and chatty guests. I circled the restaurant asking if anyone had seen a woman who looked like the mother of the bride. The bartender said that he had just "taken care of her" but didn't know where she was. I was moving quickly and did not stop to think about what "taken care of her" meant.

In desperation, I decided to check the restroom just in case. Nothing like running down people in the restroom, as my adult kids often accuse me of doing when I'm looking for them. Pushing open the door, I saw a woman with a drink in one hand and another full glass in the other. We do dividend drinks in our restaurant meaning she still had about three drinks to go. She looked at me and she was more than a little embarrassed. She said: "I guess I was wrong. This wedding thing is more stressful than I imagined. Please don't tell my kids." I told her not to worry and that I totally understood as I recently had hosted four weddings in a variety of locations for our own family. I invited her to come into the office where she could sit and slowly take the drinks, perhaps one at a time and return throughout the evening. She accepted my invitation to place the second dividend drink in the office and returned to the wedding party, but not before she gulped down the rest of the first.

Christmas at J. Arthur's.

The Missing Chef at Christmas

It was three days before Christmas, the busiest time of the year. Within a day or two we would host thousands of tourists as school was out. The most wonderful time of the year was about to happen and the weather was perfectly cold for the holidays, just below freezing with the promise of snow. If I do say so myself, J. Arthur's is nothing short of splendid at Christmas. The decorations are spectacular thanks to the generous help of Scott Neilsen and Troy Graves with their staff, Sandy and Jackie at Cabbage Rose in Maggie Valley. Working in tandem, our own incredible staff led by Marinda Darby, a woman of invincible spirit, prepares for weeks, going through and sorting decorations from our attic. My daughter, Erin, is the catalyst for this Christmas extravaganza, organizing for days. She works tirelessly directing the effort with a result that proves to be magnificent. We always pick a twenty-plus foot tree sometime in October and then plan for how Rick will get it through the double doors. This is not an easy task and I always marvel at his strength and ingenuity in getting it in and up. People are constantly asking us if it is a real tree and how we got it in. Once the restaurant is decorated, people come from miles around. I can report that, undoubtedly, it is the most extraordinary tree in western North Carolina.

This particular day everyone was in high and generous holiday spirits. I was in the office. Normally, the head chef would be coming in at 8:00 a.m. to start the prep work but it was already 8:15 a.m. and still no chef. He had been working hard and so I thought he might have overslept. By 9:00 a.m., I was greatly concerned. My son, Rick, came to me and announced that the chef's girlfriend called in sick for him. Sick? Really? Rick added that the chef was probably hung over. Upon calling his home, the girlfriend, also employed with us (never a good idea) confirmed that he had been drinking and would not be in to work. Having had this experience several months before with this chef, we knew that our chef would not be in that day nor would he be in for several days.

It was already a hectic Christmas season as the weather was great for skiing and there had been many tour groups in the area. The week before had been extremely cold and we had many families in western

North Carolina from Georgia, South Florida, and even areas of Ohio and Tennessee. We have an exciting ski area called Cataloochee which is about ten minutes down the road and it attracts people from all over the South. We were stressed to the max and used everyone who had any idea about cooking to help us out.

It was time to move to Plan B. Having this backup plan is always a necessity in our business. My son Rick, who can do anything just like his dad, would handle the kitchen. My daughter, Erin, like her mother, not known for her culinary abilities, also went behind the broiler for a short stint. As for me, I was trying to hold it all together by keeping customers happy without having to go into the explanation of being without a head chef at this time of the year. Our one saving grace was that we always closed on Christmas Day. This would give everyone at least one day off and time to regroup before coming back to work for the next nine days straight.

We survived. In fact, we thrived and it was a good experience for all. In the restaurant business it is important to be cross-trained. Many people have to be trained to do many jobs. Thank God, many of our staff have the ability to do just that, especially family members and people who have been with us for years. All four of our kids grew up in the business and were doing something in the kitchen, usually washing dishes, by age twelve. Thanks to John's insistence, they could do anything.

After the Christmas holidays, we were closed for two days. On the fourth day following New Year's, the chef showed up with every expectation that all would be well. This had been his experience after previous stints. However, this time was different. After a few not-too-complimentary words from Rick, who had covered for him for almost two weeks straight, our chef came to realize that his goose was cooked. He was advised that it would be the last time we would put up with his antics. I would like to say it was a lesson well learned for us and for him but these life lessons seem to be repetitive in this wonderful, surprising business.

The Surprise Visit

One of the many blessings (and curses) of our business is that restaurant operators are always in the public eye. Even before the days of the internet, people could find restaurateurs by looking up your business in the local phone books and finding out where you were. This I have found to be a real gift over the years as people stop by who were long ago in our lives, and we are so delighted to see them.

One day in the fall of 2011, I was working on the computer in the office with my back to the door. There were two other people in the office so when someone knocked I just kept working. A woman came through the door and said to Erin: "Does Donna Mahoney still own this restaurant?" I heard the question and thought to myself that it was someone who wanted another gift certificate for one of the many good causes in the area and I kept working, knowing that Erin would handle it. But within a few seconds of her first words, my brain started to engage, causing me to think that I knew that northern New York voice. I wheeled around only to see the beautiful face of my college roommate, Dee from Utica.

I jumped out of my seat, ran to the door, and embraced my friend of forty-plus years whom I had not seen in at least twenty years. We had simply lost touch as our lives both went in different directions with 1500 miles and much history between us. We had been in each other's weddings, shared four years of life, and known each other's families and stories, the good and the horrible, inside and out. We loved each other unconditionally, and now here we were back together. Dee had been vacationing in the Smoky Mountains with her husband, Paul, and just happened to be driving by and saw our sign. What a small miracle and a wonderful blessing.

We vowed from that day forward that we would not lose each other again. And we have not. This type of thing happens frequently in our business, with customers, coworkers, and friends of friends stopping by to say hello after years or sometimes, decades. But this time was one of those lifelong gifts that make all the long days and nights worthwhile.

Seduced by Gorgonzola

Outside of J. Arthur's at holiday time.

What You Don't Know May Hurt You

A few years back, I was standing in a long line at a local grocery store waiting to check out. I started talking to a man standing in front of me who seemed to be a pleasant, interesting-looking middle-aged person. Soon I came to find out that *Tom* was in the party planning business. I told him that I was in the restaurant business and that at the time we were running a country club as well. I thought that maybe we could network some of the work we did.

Within a few minutes, I had told him I was from J. Arthur's. He said he had been there a short while ago. Tom told me he had a great meal but that it did not end well. He said that they had an $85 bill for four people and that he thought his friend who paid the bill had properly tipped the server. As they were leaving the restaurant, the server came running after the host in the parking lot and jabbed him in the back while accusing the host that he did not tip him enough. I was horrified and hoped that others in line did not overhear our conversation. I proceeded to question him. What did he look like? How old was he? Did he really jab him?

I properly apologized and invited him to dine on us. As soon as I checked out of the grocery store, I rushed home to get to the bottom of it all. I had strong suspicions about the identity of the server, but since I'd been out of town that weekend, I didn't want to accuse anyone unjustly.

After searching the work schedule for the night in question, I found out who it was. I called the server and asked him to meet with me. I had had "discussions" with this server, whom we shall call *Kevin*. He was a great guy, but could sometimes be temperamental. He was a good person and had worked with us for a few years so it was a delicate matter. This was his second job so oftentimes when he arrived at work he was tired from working a full day at a local car dealership. In the past year he had had many temperamental "discussions" with our hostess about not getting seated with the "right parties" and when he brought this to light he always claimed to be the offended one. I could see that it was getting to the stage where customers complained about his argumentative nature frequently enough that it was hurting our business.

When I met with Kevin, I explained the situation and asked him what he knew about it. He explained that I had gotten the story all wrong. Now I knew from experience that it was certainly possible, as I had heard the same thing said by my kids many times. (I apparently suffer, in addition to many other maladies, from cognitive dissonance.) I was ready to hear his side and I would try to have an open mind.

According to Kevin, the man who was paying the bill cut Tom off but Tom never knew it. Tom was up and walking around all night. Unbeknown to his host, Tom had been ordering and adding things to his host's bill at the bar. When the host paid the check he only paid the top bill and didn't see or pay the second bar check under it. So what he thought was an $85 bill was actually a $101 bill and the money he had left for a tip went to pay the second bill. Rather than telling us, at which time we would have absorbed it, our server thought he would right this wrong by running after the host and telling him that he, Kevin, would have to pay the bill and be left with no tip. Kevin knew this would not be the case. The whole thing was a terrible misunderstanding, but regardless, the server should have brought the problem to us rather than embarrassing everyone, mostly himself, and the restaurant for such impolite behavior. It was this misunderstanding added to several others which finally led to Kevin's leaving.

We inform employees as well as guests that we will, to the best of our ability, make all discrepancies or problems right. We would much rather have handled this when it happened than have the story of the waiter who grabbed the customer's shirt for his tip fly all around the local grocery store, not to mention the rest of our close-knit town.

Erin in action.

Mickey, the Snowy Night, and the Police

Tim and I had just returned from a business trip to our restaurant in Florida. We were tired but happy to be back as it was the time between Thanksgiving and Christmas, a heavenly time to be in the cold crisp weather of Maggie Valley. We were living in a house across the street from the restaurant at the time and were asleep that evening when a light shone brightly into our window. I looked at the bedside clock and saw that it was 3:15 a.m. Being a person who sleeps with one ear awake, I immediately jumped to my feet at the sound of the car door closing. I went to the window with phone in hand and saw a car parked diagonally in the restaurant parking lot as if the person in it wanted to make a quick getaway. Although I couldn't see the door open, I could see a light and quickly called our Maggie Valley police, well respected for their quick response to emergencies. The operator asked a few questions and as we hung up I said to her, "He's leaving now so don't bother sending the police here. Tell *Jeremy* (the policeman on the chase) he's heading east." She told me they'd block off all the area. One of the many blessings of Maggie Valley is that there's only one way in and one way out so I was sure our policemen would catch him.

I woke up my husband. Tim was sound asleep and he could, and has, slept through an earthquake. (We felt a small quake in Maggie Valley in the summer of 2013.) I shook him again and asked him to follow me. I gathered my coat and ran across the street in my floral Christmas jammies with Tim following as a sheriff's car pulled in. Not caring that I was a sad sight, I opened the restaurant door with our keys. As we approached, *Sam,* from the sheriff's department, who is a friend of ours, pointed out the wet footsteps in the snow, indicating that someone was there within the last fifteen minutes and verifying that I was not hallucinating.

We opened the door and quickly walked through. He mentioned to me that the screen was missing from the front window and I responded that it had been gone for a while, probably (like our full-time maintenance man) for many years. We headed to the office and turned on all the lights. I had no concerns about cash, as there is never any cash left at the end of the night because as mentioned earlier, we

Seduced by Gorgonzola

have become a credit card business. If by some miracle it should happen that we have a little cash, it is all given away by the end of the evening as we pay our employees any credit card tips they may have received.

I was already suspecting a certain employee of this break-in. I was more concerned that he went for the liquor as there was lots of it in the restaurant. I quickly called the alarm company and after identifying myself, asked why they didn't call us. They responded that they got no unexpected opening. No opening of the restaurant? How could that be? I couldn't understand it. We hastily searched the bar and we found no evidence of anything missing. At the time, we had a chef with a terrible drinking problem and I was concerned that it was he but now I was beginning to question myself.

In the meantime, a few miles down the road, the Maggie Valley police, always vigilant, stopped a small gray car, which fit my inept description. I knew this because it was coming across on Sam's radio. Sam confirmed what I thought I was hearing from the husky mountain voices, which I don't always understand. Five armed police cars followed this older man and surrounded his car. Finally, the driver felt the pressure that he was trapped and got the message to stop the car. (I heard this whole story later — many times.) The petrified fellow finally got out of the car and was frisked and questioned by the police.

Back at the restaurant I questioned the gal at the alarm center. At this second drilling, she mentioned that someone did enter the restaurant side door for about ten minutes but it had been called in as "expected." When I asked what she meant by "expected" she said she was told that the carpet was to be cleaned and the man who does the regular midnight cleaning said he would close and would return about 3:00 a.m. after the carpet cleaners left to put on the alarm.

It was starting to hit me. I had been away and didn't get the communications. Mickey, our midnight cleaner, may have gone home and come back. This explained the wet footsteps. I looked at Sam, shamefaced for having called him here fifteen minutes before he was going off his long shift. Not only that but as I was standing there in my Christmas jammies, I realized that apparently Mickey, our dedicated eighty-year-old cleaning person, came back to lock the doors after the carpet men left and nobody told me. Since we have a management team of three people, all family members have memory lapses with regard to communication. It was our worst skill although we are getting better at it. However, no one had told me about the carpet cleaning. In the meantime on Moody Farms Road, poor one hundred thirty pound Mickey, our devoted cleaner of twenty-six years at that time, was being questioned about the break-in. I can just see him standing there, shaking, and trying to explain. They must have quickly realized that this could not be a thief. They must have put the pieces together indicating that this delightful man could not have been the criminal.

Later in the morning, I called Mickey to apologize. He explained in detail how the police had followed him and eventually surrounded his car and frisked him. He was frightened and wondered what crime he committed. Was his tag up-to-date? Did he have a light out? Was he going forty-five in a thirty-five mile an hour speed zone at 4:00 a.m.?

About a week later, Sam, the officer on the scene, came into the restaurant for dinner, calling across the dining room as he was being seated: "Nice jammies, Donna." I smiled at him, shook my head in embarrassment, and went into the office to hide until my face regained its normal color.

A Later Life Learning Experience

In the summer of 2004, we were again desperate for a head chef. We were interviewing constantly with no results. There had to be someone out there. What makes our job of recruiting difficult is that we are so seasonal. We are open seven days a week in the season and five days a week in the off-season. We let our people know this in the beginning, but for many, they cannot adjust their lifestyle or budget to work that schedule.

Finally, to my utter joy, there appeared the "perfect man," *Miguel*, who was a self-described wonder. His family was from Spain where he was born and lived until age three. They had been in the restaurant business both there and in New York and this is where Miguel gained many of his skills. He had spent many years as a culinary genius, having doubled the sales of the small restaurant he operated just outside of Washington, D.C. After contacting him by email, anonymously, the first few times, I finally gave him my name and a couple of our websites so he could learn something about us as well.

It was immediately obvious to me that Miguel was going through a late life adjustment. About sixty, divorced with a grown son and a married daughter and grandson, he was now free to travel and make his mark on any restaurant he wanted. Perhaps he would become the new, albeit older, Bobby Flay. We were most impressed with his résumé, which I, in my desperation, did not check out. I just willed it to be true. Apparently though, he checked us out thoroughly and must have figured out I'd be impressed by a résumé that included a few things like: "was the head chef for a street children's rehabilitation project." He even listed himself as a volunteer for Catholic Relief Service program to start a food program in Baltimore. But the final clincher was a copy of a picture he sent of himself, his ex-wife, and two young kids with Mother Teresa. I should have suspected this was a setup. Later it was suggested that he probably photo-shopped the picture. He also sent me pictures of his parents visiting Spain as well as a picture of him with his grandson. What a family-oriented man, I thought. Having had a family history of community involvement, I was sold. I have since learned when anybody goes this route I should do a triple check on them.

Anyhow, the deal was struck by phone and Miguel called me back with a message saying that I was the most wonderful person on the face of the earth and he would be at the restaurant in about ten days. Actually, he sent a much more encoded message than that and I had to call my daughter-in-law, Michelle, a high school teacher, for an interpretation. I didn't know if it was a good or bad thing that he was saying but she instructed me that it was very good even if unprofessional.

A few days before the start of our season, Miguel came to us looking most professional. He was an older Spanish man with a neatly groomed beard. We showed him around town and even suggested places for him to live since we had promised him expenses to move as well as a few months' rent to start his new life. Within a few days, he began work.

His job description read "working chef" but I believe he must have missed the working part. His interpretation was to direct others in the kitchen, to dine and drink with customers, and to socialize with every available female in town. Within two days, word spread in our "sneeze and a half-mile down the street they say God bless you" town and our bar was saturated with forty-plus-year-old women who had never before come into J. Arthur's.

We were recognizing that he probably wasn't going to work out for us when out of the blue he came in one afternoon and told our secretary that he would be leaving his job that day and would she please forward his check to a certain address. She was the only one there at the time and although it came as a surprise, we were not unhappy that he was leaving. I must admit I had second thoughts about sending his check. He had promised to stay the season. I thought back to John's first job in New York and completely dismissed the idea. We were out several thousand dollars, but it was worth it to be done with him. I called him the "nine-day wonder," although I'm not sure he lasted even that long. I believe in karma. He was what my dad would have called "an operator." My kids, of course, never let me forget it and attributed it to Mom's tendency to be smoked out by anyone who uttered the word "Catholic."

Corky

I had just sat down to eat a delicious top sirloin and enjoy a glass of wine with my beloved husband, Tim. We had had a long Saturday night and my feet were aching from working the floor. Looking out from my booth in the bar, I saw a young woman carrying a baby in one hand and dragging a chair with the other. It was obvious to me that she was heading toward the ladies room to nurse her little one. Having nursed babies of my own, I knew the value of privacy. She needed some peace and quiet away from the restaurant commotion.

I quickly jumped up and ran after her and asked if she'd like to nurse in the privacy of our office. As the words left my mouth, I was reminded of the endless stacks of papers and other restaurant supplies that were in the office. I also recognized that it was too late as she was already thanking me for my "thoughtful" suggestion so I had no way to back out. I led her to the office, apologized for its lack of neatness, closed the blinds, and told her that at the very least she would have privacy.

I walked out to tell my two children, Erin and Rick, that there was someone nursing a baby in the office and not to go in without knocking.

My daughter, naturally, lectured me about letting just *anyone* into the office. I told her that every once in a while you had to take a calculated chance and I mentioned that this young woman with her arms full of baby and breasts full of milk was probably not going to rip off any of our priceless files. Erin looked at me, frustrated with her hopeless mother, and knowing by this time it was too late to change things. My son, Rick, incredibly, had no objections. I had had a long night and wasn't into any more discussions of the bad decision I had made.

Having informed everyone, I sat down to my glass of Kendall Jackson and continued talking to Tim while waiting for our meal. Just as it was being served, I happened to look toward the office door when I saw our friend, *Corky*, who had just arrived after being out of town for many months. He was moving toward the office. I was aghast because I knew instantly that he would burst in without knocking. Corky had been a local for many years and had known our family very well. We were crazy about him and he was like family. He would have no hesitation about walking in without knocking. Apparently, he thought one of us was in there and so Corky, six-foot seven-inches tall, rushed into the office (kind of a Kramer-like move). The bar was still filled so I couldn't yell to him. I couldn't get out of my seat fast enough and I rushed toward the door but not before Corky had entered. Even more horrifying was the fact that when he opened the door he proceeded to step in, look at the nursing baby and mom, and began to hold a conversation with the woman. He stood there admiring the beautiful baby with absolutely no compunction or embarrassment. I arrived in the office and gave him "the loving look" which, since he was like family, he correctly interpreted as he said his goodbyes. I apologized to the young mom who laughed and said that she was becoming used to that kind of thing.

The next time I saw a nursing mother, I invited her to use the private, upstairs locked dining room.

Larry Csonka, the Anniversary Song, and Two Brides

Saturday night, October 18, 2014, was one of the busiest nights we ever had at J. Arthur's in Maggie Valley. We had stopped taking reservations early in the day and had even stopped taking call-ahead seating as we knew that the wait would be approaching ninety minutes or even more. The phone rang constantly all through the afternoon and evening. We knew we were going to be swamped with guests who had come to the mountains to see the spectacular changing of the leaves. Mother Nature did not disappoint these tourists as the weather was picture perfect and it seemed that they were all ravenously hungry after a day in the cool fresh air. During the week I had looked at the reservation book, knowing we would be busy and I noticed that we had a reservation from a bridal couple who wanted to be in a corner, away from children. That was not a problem as we had a large party booked in our loft, but still had room in a rather private corner upstairs, overlooking the dining room with all its festive fall décor.

By 5:30 p.m. my husband, Tim, was outside trying to direct people toward parking in any nearby place as our parking lot was jammed. Everyone's adrenaline was rising. The night was unfolding as predicted with an unexpected surprise around 6:00 p.m. when Larry Csonka came through the door with a party of four. When sports people or celebrities dine with us, we try to provide them privacy as much as possible, acknowledging their presence and treating them like any other of our valued guests. During our time in Maggie Valley, we have had Tommy Lee Jones, Harrison Ford, and Frankie Avalon among others dine with us.

When Larry came in, few people recognized him, which, I think, is the way he wanted it. My son, Rick, however, did recognize him and immediately told me to check out the gold Super Bowl ring. (Glory be to God, these football giants must go to finger training gyms to be able to wear those things.)

Larry was a perfect gentleman and whenever anyone went over to his table he treated them with utter respect. When he was leaving, another guest asked for a picture and he readily agreed. We were so busy that, although the thought of a picture crossed my mind many times, I could't even get to the office to get my phone.

While Larry was dining, in walked a beautiful bridal couple all decked out in their wedding apparel. Since the lobby was mobbed with people, most all of them applauded as the couple made their way to the hostess stand. I immediately saw them and motioned them through the crowd. With a great big welcoming I said that we had their table ready in a quiet corner upstairs. They were delighted that they would be seated immediately, especially when looking around the crowded lobby. The applause continued as we walked up the stairs and the people in the dining room saw the young couple. At the top of the stairs, I showed them to their table, tucked away in a quiet corner of the upstairs loft. I congratulated them once again and left.

We soon sat the party of forty upstairs and my attention was focused on them. Unknown to me, the staff was getting ready to sing "Happy Anniversary" to a couple whose friends requested this when they brought them in to dine. Their dinner was ending and the server was preparing to provide the request for the song. The server did not know that the two wives had gone outside for a cigarette while the staff was assembling and most service was being halted in order to sing the song. By the time the staff got to the table the two women had not returned. The candles on the cake were burning and the food in the kitchen was not getting any hotter so the server made an executive decision to sing "Happy Anniversary" to the two husky men at the table. Realizing they were not a couple, the whole dining room erupted in laughter as the two men each put their heads in their hands and seemed as if they wanted to climb under the table (they told us this when they left). The two wives returned, hysterical with laughter, as the staff left the table and the entire dining room was still being entertained by this slight error in timing.

About ten minutes after seating the wedding couple, a beautiful middle-aged couple came in dressed in blue jeans and said that they made a reservation for 7:00 p.m. as it was their wedding night. The woman was wearing a black shirt, outlined with diamond studs that read "BRIDE." I looked at my daughter Erin and she looked at me as if to say, "Okay, now what did you do, Mom?" I explained to the newly married bride and groom that a young couple just came in dressed as a bride and groom and that we seated them at their reserved table, thinking they were the couple who had made the reservation. At the same time, I was calculating in my mind just how long it would take before we had another table, let alone a quiet corner, virtually impossible on this busy night.

I told the second wedding couple that we would be happy to make it up to them for our mistake. My daughter quickly added discretely to me: "Whose mistake?" indicating for sure that it was mine. I sat them in the chairs right next to the hostess stand and offered to get each of them a drink. They were most gracious as they both ordered a drink, and the new bride said: "Well, I guess that if this is the worst thing that ever happens to us, we'll have a great marriage." In the meantime, everything was put on hold while I frantically looked for an opportunity to seat these two lovely people. I pointed out the only rather quiet table, also upstairs, to the couple. As I was doing this, they waved at the people who were dining at it. The second bridal couple told me that the people at the table were from Miss Caroline's Wedding Chapel and that they had just witnessed their ceremony. I knew Caroline and Burton as they are family friends and they, sitting at the table, intuitively and graciously got the message, and made the motions indicating that they would quickly finish their meal so the second beautiful wedding couple could have the table.

Within about ten minutes, the second wedding couple was seated about twenty feet across the loft from the first wedding couple still in their bridal attire. (At this stage, looking back, it occurred to me that the first bridal couple, especially the groom, did have a look of surprise when I brought them so quickly to the table. The bride probably thought that her wonderful new husband arranged it.)

To soften the blow to the second couple, I immediately told them that we would treat them to their first nuptial dining experience. It was that and more for them, as they ordered appetizers, more drinks, and the Chateaubriand for two. They were delighted at the news and thought my mistake was a fortuitous beginning to their new lives. That challenge being resolved, I returned to the lobby and the eighty still-waiting-to-be-seated people. Many were watching a fellow in the hallway having his picture taken with his friend and Larry Csonka.

And the beat goes on…

Now, tell me...how many people could possibly have this much fun on an early Saturday night in the small and hospitable country town of Maggie Valley, North Carolina?

Hope Still Springs Eternal

There is a famous restaurant in Chicago called Grace, which is owned and operated by Curtis Duffy. He began at the bottom and through many trials and tribulations ended up as one of the most celebrated chefs in our country. In constructing the story below, I feel strongly that our wonderful *Ken* will someday have a successful outcome to his life as did Curtis. My faith in him will never wane.

Each of us in our own personal and business lives has our favorites. What may be an extraordinarily wonderful person to me often appears as a joker to one of my kids or vice a versa. Why one person is attracted to another is a constant source of wonder to me and long ago I just came to realize that we each need such a variety of people in our lives. Often the same personality traits, characteristics, character or lack thereof we find charming in one person, will completely turn us off in another. Only God knows why.

Enter *Ken* who was probably and still is one of those people I'd give my life for. (Okay, this may be a little exaggerated.) A chef, who came up through the lines, he is one of the most talented, likable, and creative people I've ever met. He was also one of the most challenging in my many years of working in this business. Now I should add here that my academic degrees are in psychology, theology, and counseling. I have taught endless courses on personality characteristics and done much personality testing over the years. In my head, I knew the deal with Ken and I knew he was spoofing me the whole time. Ken was a young kid who had a substance abuse problem, the norm, unfortunately, for too many of today's promising chefs. Finding chefs who aren't afflicted is a difficult task today. I knew all the signs, indicating that Ken needed help and I tried so hard to help him. I also knew that it would probably take a life-changing event for Ken to get himself clean.

I grew up in the restaurant business at a time when most chefs were decent people trying to make a living. Actually, in our type of restaurant business, they weren't really "chefs" but rather "broiler men" back in the '50s and '60s. There used to be no need for a real executive chef. Broiler men were the people who started off as dishwashers, learned to make salads and work the line, fry potatoes, and plate vegetables. After those steps they would then grow into the position of tackling the more important items such as steaks, tidbits, filets, chops, chicken, fish, etc. As fish moved from the "for Catholics, Friday only" meal to becoming sought after in the mainstream, the country moved from beef into more creative fish, pasta, and other dishes in the '70s and '80s. It was then that the need for people who could do more than broil became apparent, at least to us. Thus the sous chef, the chef, and then the executive chef appeared to be more desirable even in "steak houses" such as ours.

But back to Ken: he became our chef rather by accident after our head chef unexpectedly left us and he remained so for about a year and a half. In spite of his great talent, keeping Ken in line was not easy. First there was his mouth which was a real problem for me. Never, to my knowledge, did we have a situation with a loud and mouthy chef who would use expletives at every second word. The first time I ever saw Hell's Kitchen with its star, Gordon Ramsay, I was in a hotel in Paris, waiting to get a flight home. I was still on a spiritual high, having attended a retreat there, after a long period of grief, and was shocked to hear the language and the disrespect on the TV show. I, who had grown up in a restaurant, couldn't imagine that any restaurant kitchen really operated like this. This was back about fifteen years ago. I came to the decision that the guys on all of our lines were not at all like that. Or could it be that they chose their words more carefully when I walked into the kitchen? I honestly believed the tone in our kitchens was much more respectable as our chefs knew from the get-go that we would not put up with verbal abuse or crude language.

Ken, however, was used to working in kitchens filled with obscenities and I was constantly on him about his language. In reality it was just his modus operandi and not given much thought by him. At the age of twenty-four, he had as much potential as anyone I had ever met. He was talented, creative, always showed up for work, and would work long hours without complaining. He loved to prepare and cook beautiful-looking dishes. His meals came out of the kitchen with love.

His personal life, however, was in shambles. His girlfriend and he broke up regularly and if they weren't breaking up they were fighting. Over the first year, we often had discussions about his personal life when there was an obvious problem but I tried not to intrude unless it effected his work.

Ken had several health problems. Some he openly spoke about (whether they were real or not) and others he tried to conceal although they were the more obvious. Frequently we would find cups of bourbon hidden in corners of the laundry room under aprons or in the walk-in coolers. I treated Ken as if he were my son taking him under my wing, having motherly talks with him about his challenges and his talents and encouraging him to clean up his act. In terms of his kitchen skills he amazed me every step of the way. Having more than a little familiarity with alcoholism, I was aware of the social retardation that occurs with it. One often remains like a spoiled twelve-year-old who will do anything to get his or her own way. Concocted stories are all part of the gig. In addition, since the addicted person finds his or her most intimate relationship with the substance they are using, all other relationships are just a farce, try as they may to make them authentic.

So for a year, we went on this way as no other shining star showed up at our door. Ken did a terrific job as chef and the meals he put out were spectacular. Everyone else was overshadowed by Ken's incredible skills. Despite all the problems, I wanted to believe the best about him.

Fast-forward to the fall of that second season with him. Fall is the most profitable time of the year for us in Maggie Valley. After October, the leaf season, it is rather quiet until the holidays so we would need to keep our head chefs at least through then. After about a year of his employment we heard the rumor that the girlfriend was pregnant. I never knew the latest details of his life as I was not on the stream of his texts to other restaurant workers nor did I want to be. I was happy to live in the state of denial as long as he showed up for work. But by the fall, Ken was reporting to me that his girlfriend was pregnant and that she would be delivering after Christmas. This was blessed news as well as troublesome as I knew he would have to do a lot of growing up in a very short time.

I believed in behavior modification. Somewhat Pollyannaish, I bought the story and counseled him regarding his fatherly duties. (I have found that my degree in counseling has been of no help with those closest to me. I have figured out it works only with people who pay.) Ken began to respond to the need to clean up his act. We sat for many long sessions; he told me his hopes for the baby and that he was reforming and going to both AA and drug counseling. He gave me specifics and I bought it all.

As time went on, he told me of his plans to move in with her parents until they could get on their feet. His partner was in a local university getting her degree in computers and all would be well. Now I should mention that the whole time I was counseling him, Erin and Rick were telling me that I was crazy and that once again, Ken was lying through his teeth. I told them both that I was ashamed of them for being so untrusting. Not all agreed with their assessment as several kitchen employees who Ken texted daily, also bought the story about the baby.

Christmas came and went and the time for the baby's delivery was just around the corner. Finally, early in the new year, Ken called me with the great news that the baby had been born and they were still at a local area hospital whose name he gave me. He sounded ecstatic. The three of them would be leaving in the morning. All was well, according to Ken, and he would be off work for a while. I was happy for him and went shopping big time knowing they would need a lot of help with the new baby as they didn't have a lot of money. Since no one believed the good news, I called the Franklin area hospital to get the birth information. Then I called the registry of births in the county. Since they were not legally married I knew only the first two names of the baby which Ken had told me but not necessarily the surname. Coming up with nothing with the first two names I assumed I had made a mistake. Certainly, he would not go this far. I awaited Ken's next call while I painstakingly wrapped the gifts.

After several days he called me and told me that they were doing great and he would be ready to start back to work soon. I told him if he didn't bring the baby over for all to see before he came back to work, to at least bring some pictures. He agreed that he would come in with some pictures of the baby. I really thought they would have been flowing all over the internet by then but I couldn't find them. By this time my kids, believing that a leopard does not change his spots, had almost convinced me that there was no baby. I wanted to believe in him so badly. Hope springs eternal. Even my husband Tim, a trained social worker and marriage counselor, said he bought the story, at least at about fifty percent. He too, had spent much time talking to Ken about becoming a father. Reality, however, was becoming obvious.

About the middle of January, Ken showed up looking incredibly good, clean, and neat, and in great shape. He said he was involved in smoking and alcohol counseling and it was working. He began with the sad story that he found out that the *phantom* child was not his and that his girlfriend asked him to move out. I said I was sorry for him and decided to let sleeping dogs lie. I'm not sure if he thought I bought the story or not; it didn't matter. I told him I thought that, all things considered, it was best for him to move on. Whether there ever was a baby or not, we had had enough drama.

He said he expected it and was thinking of getting a job in Virginia, as he had a favorite aunt there. I told him I would do what I could under the circumstances and that if he needed a reference I would focus on the positive. I also said that in spite of everything I still had hopes for him and his future. He told me that he would text me with his new phone number since we requested that the phone he had be returned to the company. A few days later he did.

The next few days we were closed. Wanting to avoid any torturous claims of "how could you be so foolish, Mom?" I went to the storeroom on one of the closed mornings and retrieved the child's gifts. I went to the store and returned the wrapped gifts. I told an abbreviated version of the story to a salesclerk who looked incredulously at me as she gave me a credit for the merchandise. I then went and bought a pair of nice boots and shoes for myself with the refund. After being emotionally involved and spending so much time with Ken and his challenges over all these months, I deserved it.

The next month, I sent him a text and told him I still believed in him. That was about two years ago. I haven't heard back…yet! Someday Ken will show up, all cleaned up. I just know it. I know it. And I will be so proud.

Just wait! **

** Please see the acknowledgments for the conclusion of this story.

The Still That Never Was and the Truck That Died

On the evening that Sandy hit Northeast United States, we were told we would have a lot of snow and wind in Maggie Valley. Expecting a big storm, Tim and I, being the restaurant's resident caretakers at the time, pulled in everything that might fly around with high winds. We walked the perimeter of the restaurant, moved many things around, and put them in the back of the restaurant. After completing that task I came in, found my scissors, and picked many of the lingering roses and wildflowers thinking how beautiful it would look having them in the restaurant. As I was finalizing my attempts, I came around to the front door of the restaurant and found my daughter, Erin, following a gentleman out the door. She, always confident and self-assured, looked rather quizzical so I asked her what was up. She said the gentleman was from the ALE (Alcohol Law Enforcement) and that he had been sent by someone in the community who had lodged a complaint that we had a still on the premises. She (nor I) had any idea of what a still looked like. She quickly and professionally told the polite but dogmatic man who was also a frequent customer that he could look for a still anywhere he wished. She was pretty sure that we were not hiding one.

When she asked why anyone would report something as ridiculous as that he responded that sometimes when a local business gets called in on the carpet for an infraction they will go on a rampage and say that other businesses are also committing the same or other infractions. As I said previously, most business people in Maggie Valley are magnificent, but as Dad would say: "Every once in a while, you get a jerk!" In any event, the gentleman did a complete and thorough check of the entire restaurant, which the ALE is required by law to do and no still was found. He knew that at the outset, but he had to fulfill his professional responsibilities.

Emergency having been handled, my son, Rick, who was off that evening, called and asked me to move our large catering truck to a

Seduced by Gorgonzola

position against the fourteen foot tall wooden fence to make sure that the wind didn't blow it off its hinges. I got the keys and tried to start the truck which had not been used in a few weeks. When it wouldn't start, Tim and I tried to jumpstart it, but no luck. Therefore I had to call Rick, who assumed it was his inept mom and stepdad (both admittedly, not mechanical) who couldn't perform the simple action. He said he'd be down to the restaurant soon.

Shortly, he arrived with his team, which included our two grandsons, John Patrick and Reilly. In Rick's mind, they were more capable at these things than we were. They tried to jumpstart the truck but again, no luck. This gave me a little satisfaction. Rick then asked if we had any ether. We didn't, so he sent Tim to the local gas station for it. Upon Tim's return, we proceeded to do other preparations while the "Rick team" worked on the truck. Within a minute or so we heard a large booming sound. I ran outside and saw the engine of the truck on fire. I yelled for the kids to get away. They ran for the water. Our hoses were too short so they had to run back and forth with water in buckets and garbage cans. For the second time in six months I called 9-1-1 for the fire department, having recently called for the fire in the laundry room. The whole situation would have been comical were it not so frightening. The emergency squad showed up within a couple minutes along with six police cars and every young rabble-rousing CBer in Haywood County who was looking for excitement. By the time everyone arrived the fire was contained and every car passing along Highway 19 was wondering what happened at J. Arthur's that warranted six police cars, emergency vehicles, and the fire department (the ALE officer's car, having just left). The snow was blowing stronger and once again I was asking myself: "How is it that I am in this crazy business at this stage in my life?"

The answer, of course, to that question is that it is in my blood. It is exciting, fulfilling, and packed with surprises at every turn. It brings me in touch with so many wonderful people and so many challenging situations. It uses every ounce of my energy although some days I just want to run and hide. On the other hand, it is an antidote to boredom. It uses all the skills that I have been trained to use and insists that I develop more each day. I certainly don't have to document any of my "cases" as I can choose to be a psychologist when I wish and just a business person at all other times. It requires new skills almost weekly because the nature of the business is constantly changing. Imagine telling John or my mom and dad about the need to be on Facebook or Trip Advisor or Twitter and about the new POS system that can give information in a few seconds that used to take Harold Hill all day to glean. The human element is what it's all about: the ability to interface each day with people from all over the world and to offer them a dining experience with great food and service, to lift them from their cares, if only for a short time, enrich their lives and create memories to last for a lifetime. Yes, life is good.

Those are the answers to the deeply philosophical and thought-provoking question I posed to myself on the night that Hurricane Sandy hit New York and the aftereffects hit our little town of Maggie Valley.

The fourth generation of Manero restaurateurs:
Rick, Erin, and Jay Mahoney.

Every exit is an entrance somewhere else.
—Tom Stoppard

CHAPTER FIVE

Manero's in Palm City, Florida

Welcome to Manero's.

This company is based on the integrity, vision, leadership, and dedication of John M. Mahoney.

That is the inscription composed by my son, Jay, and written just outside of the front door to Manero's in Palm City. We opened the latest and newest Manero's on December 28, 1998. Every single detail of the place was carefully considered by John, my husband, who had died in August of that year. He lived to see the foundation poured and some of the walls constructed, but not to see the project completed. He would have been (I believe, *is*) proud of what he planned and how our family has continued the business which he worked so hard and lovingly to develop.

The last standing Manero's, at this stage, is very different from any that preceded it. In a lovely section of Palm City (adjacent to Stuart) in Martin County, Florida, the architectural design of our building was dictated by the community planning board. It's about as different as we can imagine from 559 Steamboat Road in Greenwich or even 2600 East Beach Boulevard in Hallandale, both of which were renovated numerous times. We are often asked why the décor and the menu, among other things, are different from the Hallandale or Greenwich locations. My son, Jay, responds in this way:

> Today the Greenwich location would have been over seventy years old. Much has changed since then, even though the building did not appear to change much over the years. At one time, the waiters were all men, chain restaurants were nonexistent, and cost of food and labor was minimal. There were fewer laws and regulations and U.S. beef was not being shipped all over the world — which made it easier to get great quality. In addition to these transitions, consumer health/diet concerns and spending habits were nonexistent at the time. There are many, many reasons, but mainly this Manero's is different in an effort to provide the food, service, and environment that are demanded by the good people of the area in which we are currently located.

So, just how are we different from the Manero's of the past? Food was a lot cheaper back then. Our food costs today on some offerings exceed forty percent, which does not leave a lot of room for other expenses, not to mention profits. Expenses are higher than ever with services, insurance, liability, property taxes, and licenses at all-time highs. Government restrictions and local regulations are more invasive than ever. For example: in Palm City we are told exactly how many trees and bushes we must maintain on our premises to pass code.

Consumer health concerns, special requests, diet, and spending habits have all made our kind of dining challenging. Great food costs money and we have never been ones to cut corners in sacrificing quality. I tell people all the time we primarily serve steak and prime rib; we do not serve pizza or pasta in any large amount. In spite of all the above, the human spirit is strong, challenges are responsibly met, and Manero's and its subsidiaries continue to provide a tradition of great food, hospitality, and service with the air of sociability that could make the generations before us proud.

We are constantly changing in an effort to serve the ever-changing wants of our guests. Currently we are in the middle of a renovation at our Palm City location, in an effort to provide an atmosphere more conducive to the type of dining out that people desire today. Change in our business is constant; whether it be change of menu, type of dining, décor, or facilities. What doesn't change is our mission to serve our customers with great food and superb, friendly service. Our Manero's tradition lives on.

Sister Terry Aud Will Take Care of You

Just before we first opened our doors in Palm City, there were many challenges to be met. We were all in grief. Rick and Erin were managing J. Arthur's and all was going well there. In Florida, we were in the middle of our building project and we were under time constraints in our contract when John passed. Jay and I had to overcome constant roadblocks. As always, we spent too much money on everything; we were way over budget, and at every turn there were more unexpected outlays of cash. Having built several restaurants, we always knew to plan to be over budget by a good percentage but the restrictions and codes were making it costlier than our wildest expectations.

Dealing with the city, the water department, the gas department, the landscaping department, and all the codes was daunting. In addition, the developer from whom we brought the property demanded that every detail be to their liking down to the color and tone of the paint. I remember spending many agonizing hours with the wife of one of the developer's managers, who seemed to be working through the delusion that she was a design architect. She made my life miserable.

In the middle of all this, enter Sister Terry Aud, a well-known and respected Sinsinawa Dominican nun who worked with the poor in Indiantown. She was incredibly well thought of in the county for the work she did with the poor and migrants and she had the commissioners, town and county officials, and townspeople wrapped around her small South American finger. She was a firecracker. She spoke perfect English with a charming Spanish accent. We had known Sr. Terry for years having helped her with her fundraising events many times. She had been crazy about John and was even crazier about Jay, as he, too, had been very good to her.

One day, prior to the opening, she came in from Indiantown, about twenty miles away, for a meeting. She stopped in our soon-to-be-opened building while Jay was out. She asked how things were going for us, four months after John's death. I thanked her for her love and concern and responded appropriately. Also I told her we had had many challenges with the city, but that somehow, we would be ready for our opening soon after Christmas.

Sister Terry had a reputation of having fought with many powerful and obstinate churchmen as well as influential city and county officials to get what she needed for her projects. She was strong and determined and would not be put down by any middle manager. Never one to mince words with her most effective Spanish accent, she said: "Donna, you tell Jay, if anyone gives him trouble…" and at this point she raised her right hand and she opened and closed her fingers many times with rugged determination, and continued…"If anyone gives him trouble, just let me know and I will crunch his *cojones* to smithereens!"

Despite my grief over the loss of John, I howled with laughter. She seemed not to be able to understand why as she was dead serious in her resolve. I told her (jokingly) that I was shocked by her insinuations. I wasn't, but she loved it and we hugged and she left. I don't remember a lot of trouble with the city or county officials after that. In fact, many of them became our best customers.

Manero's of Palm City.

Working in a Restaurant

They say that everyone should work in the restaurant business at least for a while especially as a server even if he or she is going on to something different later in their lives. I completely agree with this. Being in our business is a course in life and living. It teaches you the kind of person you may want to become or the kind of person you may never want to become. During that first week at Manero's in Palm City, a few incidents stand out in my mind, again demonstrating the best and the worst in people.

We had decided to do free valet service in our parking lot. We always had this service in our restaurant in West Palm Beach and people loved it. We also offered people the ability to park themselves if they preferred. On the second night of our opening, we were tested in this. We were swamped with guests wanting to try a new restaurant (my advice always being to wait a few weeks for them to get the kinks out). We had two sons of close friends who were available to work for a few days as they were home from school over the holidays. One was in college and the other was finishing his last year in law school. When one customer got out of his car that night, he was so upset at the prospect of valet parking and having to tip the valet (even though he also could have parked in the lot) that he threw the keys on the ground and said: "Okay, kid, if you want them, pick them up!" Chip Poncy, then a great kid who went on to become an incredible public servant fighting terrorism and who gives me a glimmer of hope for the U.S. government, never flinched and just said: "Yes, Sir."

On that same night we had a party of twelve, the Skowroneks, from Palm Beach Gardens who waited, with their children, for over an hour to get a seat. When they left, every single member of their family said "thank you." The grandfather, Peter, added that it was one of the best nights and meals of his family's life.

I remember a party of three who were high on themselves. They had read of our opening in the morning press and they called me over and questioned me as to why we didn't do things like a variety of restaurants in New York City that they frequented. They were insulting and arrogant and after several attempts to make them happy, I simply told them that if they were not satisfied with our food and service, we would be happy to pick up their check. They continued to complain but ate it all and then took me up on my offer. I was delighted to get them out of the restaurant as there were many people waiting for tables. I am reminded of Anthony Bourdain's words: "If anything is good for pounding humility into you permanently, it's the restaurant business."

In those early weeks, two older customers still stand out in my mind and heart. They had come because they had heard so much in the news about Manero's. They said that they waited six months for our opening and had been planning a special night out for weeks. They brought us flowers and told us of their delight that we were in the community. They have been with us every Sunday night since. Overall, the opening went extremely well, except for the few situations mentioned. Unfortunately, it is often those you remember. Once again Dad's "every once in a while, you get a jerk" phrase flowed through my head. But for every hundred customers who come to our restaurants, ninety-nine of them are absolutely delightful.

The Fire Alarm

One of the most problematic issues of our newest Manero's was the fire alarm. For some reason, not known to mortals, the fire alarm, especially in our earlier years had a need to go off on our busiest Saturday nights in the middle of the season, usually about 7:30 p.m. I remember one Saturday in particular. Jay was gone, probably working a party at another location, and Joyce, Kathy, and I were the team on the floor. It was extremely busy and we had a long line of people waiting, many of them from New York and other parts of the Northeast.

Regarding the fire alarm, we had been doing some renovation in our dining room to alleviate a noise problem that was causing customers to complain. Renovations always called for a lot of movement of electrical lines. Apparently when some of the work was done, wires got crossed and that was the cause of the sporadic firing of the alarm. Since it was a Saturday we were closed for lunch and only a few of us were there. The alarm company had been working on the problem and we thought they had solved it. So when the alarm started to go off after they left, we felt there was no real fire, but just to be safe we cleared the lobby. Our part-time sous chef, who was a fireman in his other job, checked it out for us. With no fire or problem detected after his inspection, I tried to remain calm and cool and to reassure the customers. Guests had been looking to us for direction but few had moved from their tables so I began informing people that we believed it to be a false alarm but that they were welcomed to go outside if they wished. The fire department was coming for confirmation.

Dinner continued to be consumed as almost no one went outside, despite the noise that ensued. This amazed me as few seemed to be concerned and most of our guests went chatting away with their friends. Meanwhile, firemen arrived and remained for the next half-hour, while the alarm continued blaring intermittently. At about 8:00 p.m. the fire alarm technicians came in and disconnected the lines. They stayed until late into the night fixing the problem.

All I remember about the night is that we served many complimentary desserts as well as complimentary glasses of wine to compensate people for the disturbance during their meals. The whole evening would have been comical were it not such a potential disaster. I remember going home, being drained, and asking myself again how I ever got to where I was. It was not one of the best nights of our new restaurant's life.

Michael Riccitello

I shall never forget an early morning phone call I got in 2002. My son, Jay, like me, an early riser, phoned about 5:00 a.m. and said only "Mike's gone." Since I had just awakened, I couldn't quite get my head around the thought he was trying to convey. "What do you mean *Mike's gone?* Did he quit? What happened?" Still in shock himself, he told me Mike had died. Michael Riccitello was an employee of our restaurant in West Palm Beach for many years and then followed us to Palm City. He had been a cautious and avid motorcyclist so it was a double shock to learn he had been struck by someone who had a medical emergency on the road just two miles from the restaurant. It was unthinkable and especially since Mike and his wife, Aino Kay, had just completed a 10,000-mile trip around the country without a scratch on that very cycle.

Mike was a smart, quick-witted, and customer-friendly kind of guy who came from Upstate New York. He had worked there in his family's business where he learned the art of managing a great bar. He had time for everyone, knew just how long to stay before moving on, just how much to say without crossing boundaries, and exactly how much each customer could drink before saying good-night. He'd greet everyone with a "how war ya" or "what's up, Jerry?" in his delightful Upstate New York, Italian kind of way.

His loss was a terrible adjustment for restaurant employees and patrons. His wake was filled with customers who had come to think of him as one of their own family. He was not only an employee but was like family to us and a brother to Jay as well. We miss him still today and we have since renamed the bar the "Riccitello Lounge" in his honor.

Manuel

At one time, a view into our kitchen would be a lesson in American assimilation. The integration of cultures always made things interesting in the kitchen, as one would have to either know a few words in a variety of languages or be skilled at speaking with one's hands. The variety of languages spoken in our Florida kitchen on any given night is amazing, with Spanish being the basis of many of them. All the Mahoney kids have Spanish language skills but my choice of Italian as a preferred foreign language does not always help that much. (My husband Tim, who is fluent in Gaelic, which is not a big help either, believes that speaking in English and exaggerating every word very slowly should make him understood by anyone of any background. This, I keep telling him, is not the solution.) In any event, honest mistakes take place when ice cream is ordered and the ticket is read by someone who interprets it as onion rings.

Over the years of being in the restaurant business in Florida there has been a subtle shift in kitchen staffs, as fewer and fewer American-born citizens seem to be drawn to basic kitchen work. To try to adjust to these kinds of challenges, I have come to realize that Jay, when he hires whether by happenstance or design, will hire several people of the same culture, one of whom has English language skills and who can relay translations to some of the others whose skills are not that great. Perhaps this is not always planned but still it happens as a sous chef will have an uncle who has a cousin who has kids, all of whom fancy restaurant work.

Manuel was a person of Hispanic background who came to us as a chef. He was from Central America and had been in the States for many years as had many of his relatives. He was a superb chef and ran a well-organized kitchen and put out beautiful meals. Manuel just had one problem, as far as I could tell from an employer's point of view, but it was a serious one. He loved to drink. Manuel never came in drunk, never came in late, and never displayed some of the other habits of people with similar problems, however he did end up in jail after his third DWI. This presented a big problem for our kitchen as, first of all, he was the one who spoke the language, an offshoot of Spanish, and did the translations, and secondly, since four of our kitchen staff who worked there were driven to work by him, they had no other way of getting to work. So for the three days that Manuel spent in jail, Jay had to provide transportation to and from work for these coworkers or our kitchen staff would be down to about three. Jay also had to fill in as the part-time chef for a short time. Thankfully, that was one of the skills he learned not only at the right hand of John Mahoney but also while studying for his Master's Degree in Restaurant Management.

Manuel returned from his stint in jail, with a stern warning from Jay that this would be his last time he would go down this path. If he had another DWI, Jay would fire him as the disruption of the kitchen was just too much to handle. The warning was heeded for at least six weeks, after which Manuel had another DWI. This time it meant that he would be going to jail for an extended period of time, so there was no question that we would need not only a new chef but probably a whole new kitchen staff as communicating with Manuel's relatives was not that easy for the remaining chefs and workers.

As a result of the DWI, Jay did let him go, and his search for a new chef began again. We soon heard that rather than going to jail, Manuel had changed his identity and his address and was working as head chef at a local Oriental restaurant, along with his relatives. And so it goes, and so it goes, and…

I Do Not Cook

When John died and we reopened Manero's in the new location in Palm City, I recognized that I had become the matriarch of what would soon be the last two surviving Manero's restaurants. In that position I found it necessary to admit the following: I do not cook!

I know you may think I'm exaggerating but ask my family and they will tell you. Oh yeah, I kept skin on my kids' bones when they were young, but you really wouldn't call it cooking. I did hamburgers, hot dogs, sloppy Joes, and pizza. Occasionally I tried lasagna but gave up on it when our kids wouldn't even eat it saying that it was burned. Then I tried my mom's spaghetti and meatballs recipe, a specialty in our family. That was pretty good but it would take hours to make and I was not that patient when I was younger. I still am working on that.

My sons, Jay and Rick, who cook, and Tim, my beloved, who does incredible eggs!!

The men in our family cooked. When I was young, my dad cooked. Even my brother, Peter, cooked. When I married John, he did most of the cooking, and now, thank God, our sons and sons-in-law cook. Actually today, even our grandsons cook. Extraordinarily well. And I must add that the superb woman cook in our family is our daughter, Shannon, who must have gotten the "cooking" gene from John. Other than Shannon, it's a male trait, but I'm sure you think I'm kidding. How could a sixty-plus-year-old woman grow up in the restaurant business and not cook, you ask?

Well…honestly…I just don't know. I had no need to cook back then as our family ate most of our meals at the restaurant and I just "supplemented." I always did everything in the front end of the house: the administration, the hospitality, the advertising, bookkeeping, customer relations, advertising, promotions, payroll, costing of food, but mostly stayed out of the kitchen, until recently.

When customers asked me how things were made I'd check with John or with the chef in the kitchen. I had no earthly idea. So now you know. I am no Rachel Ray or Giada and obviously, I'm not the Barefoot Contessa. But just in case you don't believe me, here are a few instances.

In high school I had to take a year of home economics. One part covered sewing, and as my mom was a professional seamstress by training, I did well in that. The second semester dealt with cooking. Now I was a good student, but I believe that one semester was one of those that I was not on the honor roll. It was not because of physics, which I loved, but rather, home economics.

When I first married and my father-in-law came to visit us, he wanted English toast. I didn't know English toast had to be "toasted" and I put it in the warming oven without slicing it. Soon after, my mother-in-law came (they traveled separately) and to add insult to injury, when I was working in the restaurant one night, she fed the kids at home. She was a delightful woman and I loved her like crazy. She took what she could from the refrigerator where she found some Jell-O for dessert. Trying not to be too critical she told my kids upon having a hard time with the rubber: "Now next time, dears, tell your mother to stir the bottom of the Jell-O before chilling it." Jell-O!

And then there were the endless affronts by friends. At many church parties, unless John was coming the word was always: "And we decided to have you bring the wine, Donna; you don't have to cook anything." They thought it was a well-meant and kind effort to keep the congregation from food poisoning.

But the final embarrassment which changed my life happened about ten years ago. My beloved friend, Marnie, a great cook, was preparing a dish to be served at my home in Palm City, soon after we opened the restaurant. It was a shower for a family member. It was a Saturday morning and she was frantic to get rosemary. She asked me if I knew of any place on the way to my house, and being a tabula rasa on herbs and spices, I said: "Not really, Marn, but you can try the Publix near me on the way over."

To her delight she did get it at Publix only to arrive at my house, put on her apron, and go to the sink and find rosemary growing in the window. She looked at me with both irritation and compassion (as only she can do) and said to me: "Donna, do you know what this is?" I knew it was a lovely aromatic herb, but no, I didn't realize it was rosemary.

Seduced by Gorgonzola

Me, Tim, and Marnie Poncy

Having just lost John, with both my sons on their own, I realized that I was going to have to learn at least a little about cooking if I was going to survive as the matriarch of Manero's and if I were to (at long last) obtain a reputation of culinary competence with my friends. Moving from the front office into knowing as much as possible about everything about the kitchen (which I still don't) is a job that's been taking me some time.

My neural pathways have been hard to correct on this journey. I am trying to catch up to others with my culinary skills. I educate myself with many trips to our chefs to query them about the ingredients in our dishes and the actual cooking methods used. I have become quite knowledgeable about the meals that we serve. Today I can tell you what every single herb and spice is (I will not be embarrassed by rosemary again), and in what it can be used. In fact, Tim and I have a beautiful herb garden behind the restaurant that we share with other restaurants in the community. I have come a long way in ten years.

However, still having those feelings of inadequacy when it comes to these areas of culinary competencies, if you come to any of our establishments and ask me *exactly* what is in the chicken marsala, just hold on a minute.

I'll get right back to you.

Who's got the Keys?

Recently at lunchtime in Palm City we had two lovely women guests. The gals each had a drink, maybe two, as they engaged in a long conversation, while sitting in the lounge. After being filled to the brim and having discussed all the things that were important in their universes, they got up to leave. They left a tip for the server and went out to the front lobby, thanking Joyce. One of them, the supposed driver, began searching for her keys. Joyce, who can calm all troubled waters, recognized that the woman was a little wobbly and that she shouldn't be driving even when she did find the keys. So Joyce quietly said to the friend, in much better shape, that maybe she should drive the car. The friend gave Joyce a knowing nod, indicating that she would be driving as I'm sure that she had no intention of letting this woman get behind the driver seat if she were in the car.

A few minutes passed and she still couldn't locate the keys after having dumped everything out of her purse onto our front desk. She then proceeded back to the bar and asked the server what she (the server) did with the keys which she now was sure were on the table when she left. The server said there were no keys but the woman insisted that she must have left them there so the server went behind the bar to get a flashlight to thoroughly check under the booth. Still no keys and the woman was more convinced than ever that they were in the garbage. The server, certain that there were no keys left on the table, checked the bus pans and the garbage that she recently had placed in the can, thinking that, thankfully, the new trash bag was placed in the can within the last fifteen minutes. The woman was getting uncontrollable as she was convinced that someone had stolen her keys and would drive off in her Highlander to parts unknown.

Joyce, always calm and a master at handling situations such as this, quietly invited the friend to take her companion to the bench outside the door. She was hoping the guest would settle down while she tried to figure out how to: a) find the keys as she obviously got to Manero's somehow and b) get them out of the restaurant so the remaining customers would not witness the debacle. She told them that she would call them a cab and that we would pay for it, hoping that the woman had another set of keys at home. The woman who owned the car was hysterical by this time, but the friend, embarrassed by her friend's behavior tried to make everything okay between us and her friend.

After Joyce got them seated outside, she asked the friend where the car was, thinking perhaps that the woman dropped them on the way to the restaurant. This sometimes happens and other guests will pick them up and bring them in. Joyce wended her way out to the car, only to find the windows down, the car unlocked, and the keys in the ignition. The keys extracted, Joyce handed them to the friend who thanked her profusely as she helped the wobbly friend into the front passenger seat. Problem solved, customer happy, and Joyce went back to the front desk with another great story to tell her grandchildren.

In our business, the customer is (almost) always right.

From Our Side: A Sample Day in the Life of Manero's

When people make a name for themselves in the field of sports or entertainment, one of the first things many of them do is to find a business partner with whom they open one (or many) restaurants. This arrangement has always amazed me and I stand in wonder of anyone who thinks that the utter adrenaline flow which exists on any given day is a good substitute for somewhat of a normal and peaceful life. Do they have any idea what they are getting into?

Think of Jennifer Lopez, Kenny Rogers, Don Schula, Dale Evans, Magic Johnson, Steven Spielberg, Kevin Costner, Ted Turner, and an endless list of others. Even CNBC's Jim Kramer owns a restaurant verifying for me his total lack of stability. Doesn't being involved in the stock market provide Jim with enough euphoria and depression to satisfy his need for craziness? Still, he does it and we still love you, Jim.

On any given day at Manero's in Palm City, I am amazed by the happenings. It is a perfectly orchestrated three-ring circus in which the leader, Jay Mahoney, is assisted (and sometimes led) by Joyce Thomas, and supported by the great staff of Danielle, Pam, and Kathy and the team at the epicenter.

Let me walk you through a sample day: Jay shows up about 7:00 a.m. The morning starts with the party in the back room. It's a breakfast for marketers — a group that comes together once a month to share their success stories and help each other. They start coming in around 7:45 and the last person leaves about 9:30 after having had a breakfast buffet. Upon their departure, our housekeeper, and a team of servers, get the room cleaned up for the next group which will arrive at 11:30.

Meanwhile in the office, a team that serves at a local club we operate, is getting ready for the day. The club has limited kitchen and refrigeration capacity so all the luncheon sandwiches and salads are prepared at Manero's. We never know if there will be thirty or seventy so flexibility is essential. They get prepared, packed up, and leave around 10:00 a.m. for their twelve-mile trip. If anything is forgotten — which it sometimes is — someone needs to return to Manero's to pick it up.

The Manero's food van — quite different from the first one.

The food van, which serves a limited menu in downtown West Palm Beach, is getting loaded up to make the thirty-mile trip down I-95 for a three-hour period where they serve our famous food to the West Palm Beach community, near where we had operated our restaurant for twenty-eight years. The team has to be on the road by 9:00 a.m. as they usually have a catering drop-off at one of the businesses or professional groups in West Palm Beach.

In the meantime, the kitchen begins to prepare for lunch. Today the Kiwanis will be in the main dining room. They start coming in around 11:00 a.m. although the meeting is at noon. The back room will host the Michigan Retired Teachers today. They will have forty or fifty men and women to plan their community service and to stay connected to each other.

Back in the office, we are planning ahead to purchase all that is needed for the B and A Market — a business in which we serve fast food every Saturday and Sunday. We have a team of ten to fourteen employees there every weekend at 7:00 a.m. to serve simple but tasty food to those who want to eat a bite while walking around and shopping.

Meanwhile, in the office, phones are ringing, salespersons are greeted, a gas leak is being looked into, and Joyce tries desperately to make a few entries into QuickBooks. The meeting with the accountant is next week and with all the interruptions, it will take a miracle for her to be ready. Soon it will be 11:00 a.m. and time to open the doors for the two luncheon groups who always come early. In addition, a team of servers is doing the prep work for our regular lunch customers, most of whom use the lounge or the alcove.

The to-go orders start to come in about this time too. On any given day there is catering for office groups, anywhere from one to three groups of a variety of sizes in addition to a variety of smaller orders we take over the phone or by fax.

The public opening begins and the action shifts to the front desk and kitchen. Generally the parties are groups for whom we can prepare but there is no telling how many will be in for lunch. The whole staff is in a constant state of awareness and the ability to shift gears on a dime is essential. Behind the scenes, many things happen of which few guests are aware. One of the chefs has called in sick and a server has a sick child. Plan B is put into effect. Those who were to be at the desk may be doing double duty today.

The beat rolls on. Lunch is successful. The groups disburse and a few people linger at the bar and in the back room. Eventually, we reset the back room for an afternoon funeral party at three o'clock. The gals and guys arrived back from the club, and if it's a Tuesday or Friday, the next group plans to go out and serve dinner there. The lunch staff goes home and the office staff grabs a quick bite between the phone ringing and the constant knocks at the door.

Some, including Jay, have children to be picked up before it all starts again for the evening. The dinner crowd will be different so another type of preparation begins. Soups, sauces, and gravies are prepared. Fresh vegetables and beef are cut and the prime rib is in the Shaam oven. It is the Manero's experience. On any given day at Manero's, the hours are long; the details endless; frustration is the name of the game; you have got to be crazy or brilliant. It's in our blood and the magic of it all keeps us moving forward.

From Our Side: A Sample Night

The nights at Manero's are different from the days. Guests are not in any rush. Many still want the complete Manero's experience starting with a glass of wine. Most want to take their time enjoying it, a dining experience rather than a meal. We aim to please. Often they will start off at the bar and then move to their table within a half-hour or so. Others stay at the bar enjoying the sociability of their partners or friends. Gorgonzola cheese salads are served by the dozens, dividend drinks are ordered, and the night rolls on. Since it is the middle of January and it's expected to be busy, the chef and kitchen staff gear up for a whole new shift coming for the evening.

Like so many guests I have spoken to over the years, a friend and guest, Patricia Pavelka, remembers the Manero's experience from when she was thirteen years old and has repeated it many times over with her family. She wrote us:

> My love affair with Manero's Restaurants began when I was thirteen years old and at sixty-six years of age,

it continues to be as strong as ever in my palate and in my heart.

It all began when I first met Donna Tiernan at Hallandale Park. She invited me to her home where I met her mom and dad and of course her brother, Peter, all of whom were welcoming. During the course of the evening, Donna asked Peter if he wouldn't mind getting us dinner from downstairs. About forty-five minutes later, Peter came up with Gorgonzola salad, a huge loaf of garlic bread and prime rib. When I took my first bite of Gorgonzola my love for their food became addictive and I have been hooked ever since on the famous cheese salad and fabulous fresh flavor of their food, such as the succulent, tender juicy steaks, ribs, and fresh salmon.

I have just returned from Manero's in Palm City and once again I was so impressed by the outstanding customer service and most importantly, their delicious food.

Like Patricia, many come to Manero's today for the same reasons they have been coming for almost seven decades. They love the food, and our aim is to give them great service and a real comfortable place to dine with friends and family.

The Bar

The bar at Manero's is a popular place. In the season it is brimming with people sitting, and a second or third row standing behind the first. This is what we love to see.

Dee and Mike stop in for a drink before they host a group of people who they will be taking to the Kravis Center in West Palm Beach. They have been friends of ours for years and they own a successful travel business. They will be meeting their bus drivers and clients a few blocks away before making the thirty-mile trip to West Palm Beach. They are always asking Tim and me to come along on one of their trips, and of course we plan to should life ever get a little more subdued for us.

Cecil comes in to the bar to pick up "chicks." Cecil is around fifty-five and the chicks can be any age from thirty to sixty. He is constantly telling our staff to keep on the lookout for women who might be available. He is a divorced man and lonely but no longer wants to hang out in the "teenybopper bars" with dozens of guys all vying for the same younger girls.

Porky G., a well-heeled gentleman, walks through the door and tells us for the hundredth time that he is from Villa del Aqua, a wealthy community in the neighborhood. He would like a quiet booth in order to entertain his friends. When we first moved here, everyone from this community introduced themselves as being from Villa del Aqua. They must have been indoctrinated into this method of promotion. Porky comes in about twice a week always reminding us where he is from and how wonderful it is there. We love him. We know him well enough now that when he enters we kiddingly say: "Hi there, Porky from the Villa!"

Mike, Tom, and Barry come in for a drink and to watch the evening news together before having dinner. They talk about stocks and options, puts and calls, their business deals, their kids, their golf games, and their former or current wives. These guys have been meeting together on a twice weekly basis for three years. They are a sociologist's dream in terms of how they support each other.

In the corner booth is the chairwoman of a large family corporation who is as delightful as can be. During the season, she comes in weekly with a friend of hers who runs her farm not far from here. During the summer months she spends her time on Fire Island.

It's spring training season, and we get several of the managers from the major league teams. They are far enough away from base that everyone will not be expecting them to be here and won't be bothering them throughout their meals. Golfers come in for dinner after their games at one of the areas many great courses. They review their games with each other; talking about the putt they missed by an inch and the fact that the greens are not being kept the way they used to be. Oftentimes they meet their spouses or partners for dinner after drinks.

Some people are concerned about the station we have on the TV in the bar. There is a constant struggle between CNBC and FOX news and all night long the remote is moved back and forth depending on who has the loudest voices at any given time.

The place is buzzing; a restaurateur's dream. Jay walks through the bar with his apron on, stopping to say hi to everyone. Most of these people have been coming in for years and he has become friends with many. He converses easily and listens to advice, family concerns, problems, stock picks, what's happening in the community, and in the world. He takes it all in, giving his input in his personal, humorous, and unique way. He is analytical, concerned, and warm in his responses, jumping to no conclusions but not missing a trick. He is a Manero/Tiernan/Mahoney offspring for sure.

Dining Room

In the dining room, on any given night at Manero's, *Mrs. Lee* is coming in with her party of six but she will only sit at a round table. By the time her party arrives at 6:15 p.m., the time for the early-bird dinner has passed. Mrs. Lee misses the early bird and the round tables are all gone, due to a mistake in communication. She is really upset, but our hostess, *Carlie*, gets her back into her good graces by telling her that we have her favorite entrée, pork osso bucco, as a special tonight. All is well.

On this night a delightful surprise occurs when we recognize Chi Chi Rodriguez coming in the door. Chi Chi is easy-going and unassuming, and very agreeable when one of our staff asks for a picture of him before he leaves. He is frequently in the area and we are happy to take good care of him. All through dinner, people smile and wave and a few stop by to say hello. As always, he speaks to everyone with enthusiasm and intent, and he doesn't forget to summon the server for the picture before he leaves.

Several couples have made reservations for booths in the dining room, as booths have become our most popular seating. Booths seem to provide intimacy, which many couples or even foursomes want. We have many booths and they always seem to be the first to be taken. Guests have no problem when we tell them there is a wait for one and will sit and gaze at other guests as they dream of their dividend drink, shrimp cocktail, Gorgonzola, and their prime rib.

Long-time residents from some of the many clubs in the area are assembling their parties of four, six, and eight for a meal they "have been waiting for all week." Many of these people are known by first names as they have been coming to Manero's for years.

The younger hostesses, when they first come to work for us, are always amazed at the number of people who will wait for a half-hour or more to get the exact table or server they want. Many of our guests have favorites, although we hope and train all our servers to be gracious and customer-service oriented.

We are always attracting new guests and especially families who have moved to the area and have heard about Manero's. There are specialties of the house every night, and all day long the phone will ring with guests trying to find out what those specialties are. The dining room is abuzz with activity and all are happy. Customers leave with their tummies filled and with happy hearts. Our servers are delighted with business. This is the season (or the "sizzin") in South Florida at Manero's. It's busy and it is hard work but it is exhilarating.

Ribs in a Jacket

As mentioned earlier, over the years we have had a lot of the sports reporters or trainers dining at Manero's as the teams they follow or train are in nearby towns along the Treasure or Gold Coast. They usually sit back and have a couple of drinks and a huge steak or prime rib. This night however, one of them, *Davey*, decided to have our baby back ribs, a succulent dish that usually is served with enough ribs for two meals. During the course of the evening, Jay, who knows most of this group, stopped by their table in the lounge to chat for a minute and recognized that Davey and friend may have had too much to drink. He offered to take them back to their hotel, a twenty-minute ride from the restaurant, and they, recognizing that they may have overimbibed, agreed. It was a busy March evening, and Jay went back to the kitchen to make sure all was under control as he'd be gone from the restaurant about an hour in total while transporting them. In addition, he had to get a bus person who would follow him in another car so he could get back to the restaurant.

Seduced by Gorgonzola

In the meantime at the bar, Davey was getting antsy and was ready to leave. He had asked the server for a to-go box to take home the rest of his ribs, but when she didn't come back immediately, he decided to take matters into his owns hands. He placed the ribs in his linen napkin, and then thinking that would solve the problem, he wrapped the napkin with his cashmere jacket, which he had taken off during dinner, and went with his associate to the lobby to wait for Jay. By the time Jay showed up with the busboy, who would follow him in his car, he looked at Davey, and reacted immediately, thinking he had been shot! The ribs bled through the napkin and through the jacket he was holding against his chest and the sauce was dripping down into his pants.

When Jay asked what happened, Davey, a little dazed, didn't know what he was talking about. Within a few seconds, Jay realized that the bleeding was from the baby back ribs, not from Davey's ribs and he proceeded to get him out of the lobby and into the car. Jay took them back and got them safely into their suite at the hotel. The first thing that Davey did when he got to the room was to flop on the bed and he was out like a light. Jay put the ribs, along with the cashmere jacket into the refrigerator, said goodnight to the other gentleman and left.

The following week Davey came in again and Jay asked him how he enjoyed those ribs. His response, after a few expletives was to chuckle and to say: "They were great, Jay, but think I'll try something without barbecue sauce tonight!"

Kathy Przelski

Most restaurateurs would thank their lucky stars for a person like Kathy. We do. Kathy Przelski has been with us since the kids were young. She and Joyce Thomas were John's right arms in terms of a support system amidst years of employees and guests coming and going. Today they provide the same professional service for Jay. Between the two of them, they have satisfied our every need for associates who knew how to do just about anything and often do. Many others have come and gone, but the two of them have been with us through it all.

Kathy was a full-time teacher before starting with us. She has incredible organizational skills and sees details. There has never been a crisis that she could not handle. Whenever we had a large party to be catered off premises, it was almost always Kathy who was in charge. She anticipates every need that we or our guests may have and literally hundreds of parties outside of our restaurant have gone off without a hitch because of her. Over the years Kathy has catered every type of party and benefit.

Kathy has a great memory and cheerily welcomes guests by their names. She knows exactly what people want and remembers their favorite server, their favorite table, their favorite drink, and entrée. Little gets by her. Kathy is strong but fair, much like John was, taking no guff from anyone. Also like John, she is kind and gentle with people in need. She was his alter ego in Manero's in West Palm Beach, and after John died she followed us to Palm City where she has been with us for many years. When Jay cannot be there, she runs a tight ship. Now on a part-time basis, she has been one of the reasons for our success over these many years. The school system lost out but we gained an incredible asset and loyal friend when Kathy Przelski joined our team. We remain ever grateful for the blessing of Kathy in our lives.

Amazing

One afternoon, Tim and I were sitting in the back of the lounge in Palm City. I had been working in the office and Tim had been running some errands for the restaurant. We both decided that it was time to eat. It had been a busy lunch but was beginning to clear out and only two booths other than ours were filled. Across the aisle about three booths from us were two elderly ladies, probably in their eighties. One had gone to the restroom and had just returned. They had had a good old time, laughing and obviously enjoying each other's company. I love to see people having fun, knowing that for many, their time out is something they look forward to, especially when they are older and living alone.

They were leaving the restaurant and shoving out of the booth when one of the ladies knocked over her purse. Flying out of her purse and onto the lounge floor were every last Tampax and Kotex that our housekeeper had placed in the ladies room for the use of our guests. The woman, not flinching, bent down slowly and picked them up. I was in a state of hysteria thinking to myself what does an eighty-year-old woman do with Tampax? I was reminded, once again, that this was South Florida. Someplace, there would be a valuable market for these goods.

The False Teeth

Like all businesses, our Manero's in Palm City Florida has changing demographics depending on the time of the year. In addition, the different rooms in our restaurants attract different people. The bar however has a fairly well-integrated group of women and men from early twenties to about eighty-five. One never knows or can predict what might happen with people frequenting the bar. For example, there are people who will only come into the bar when we have a certain bartender. Some like men. Some like women. Some prefer older bartenders and others like younger ones. Younger people do not necessarily like younger bartenders and vice versa. It's a never-ending task trying to make people happy. I have frequently had the telephone ring only to be asked the question: "Is Josh on tonight?" or "Who will the bartender be tomorrow night?" It's a constant source of amazement.

One evening we had an unknown middle-aged guest come in with her husband and family of two young adult sons. After having one drink at the bar, they sat down in a booth. Although we are careful about how much alcohol we serve people, this woman must have had a low tolerance or else she was ill. Or…maybe she had been drinking before she came to Manero's. After eating, she went to the restroom and got sick. It was obvious that something was wrong with her as she was gone from the table for some time and her family asked us to send someone in to ask if she was okay. She said yes and soon she came out and left with her family.

The next morning it was determined that the ladies room toilet was plugged and we called the plumber who came and cleaned the lines. We paid the $85 bill and thought the problem was solved. By evening, however, it was determined that the toilet still was not properly functioning. So again the following morning we called the plumber. We and the plumber were pretty upset that the work he did was not sufficiently adequate. He used a huge router to redo the job.

Lo and behold. Unbelievable! What did the plumber find? It was none other than a pair of false teeth that had been clogging up the toilet. We were all aghast. Who could possibly have flushed their false teeth down the toilet? Our plumbers have had to fish out keys, cell phones, and even, in our Maggie Valley restaurant, a four-inch diameter checker that came from our checker game in the lobby. We have paid a lot of plumbing bills for things that I won't mention here, but never for a set of false teeth.

The strangest thing was that it was five days after the event that a woman called and asked if we, by any chance, found her false teeth. We told her that we had found them. She asked if she could come over and get them and we told her: "Yes, of course." The whole time we were discussing amongst ourselves who in the world would ever place false teeth from a restaurant toilet back in her mouth. An hour later a woman showed up and collected her false teeth (minus the check for the $195 worth of plumbing services) and thanked us. Who was it but the woman who had been in the lounge with her family five nights before.

Strange, but we never remember seeing her again.

The Executive Soup Chef

Not too long ago, Jay hired a well-credentialed executive chef for our restaurant in Palm City. *Chef Judy* came to us with all kinds of recommendations and did an exceptional job. Every plate left the kitchen garnished as if it were plated up by a professional for her final exam at the Culinary Institute of America and for about three months all were delighted with her. She seemed to be a pleasant person and occasionally would bring her son in to work with her. The boy would remain with her until his dad got off work. Judy was pleasant and easy to get along with and we were sure that she would be with us for many seasons.

All was going well until one early morning around three o'clock when Jay got a phone call from the alarm company who said that there had been an opening and that they had sent the police to the restaurant. As mentioned earlier, since there is never any cash in restaurants anymore, there would be little reason for someone to break in, unless they were stealing products. When Jay arrived he saw a familiar-looking car in the back of the kitchen in addition to three police cars. He unlocked the doors and walked through the kitchen only to find Chef Judy, a little foggy looking, with a couple of glasses and a bottle of bourbon. A number of pots were lying around her as she claimed she was making the soup for the next day. We start early with our cooking — but not at 3:00 a.m. *and* we do not use bourbon in any of the soups that we currently make.

Jay told Chef Judy to call her husband to pick her up, as she was in no position to drive. Judy said she couldn't do that so Jay called her a cab and sent her on her way. Jay told her to come and see him the following afternoon after she had slept a while. Jay thanked the police, locked up the restaurant and went home, concerned that it was the middle of the season and knowing it would not be easy to find a great chef for the rest of the season. The next afternoon Judy came in with her son (good move, Judy). Jay sent the son with a server to get some ice cream in the kitchen. In the meantime, Jay, having little tolerance for these things, dismissed her immediately.

Since everyone in the kitchen had a variety of skills, the restaurant survived that season, executive chef-less, and once again we were back to square one in terms of finding a leader of culinary arts.

Jay with Joyce and Kathy, two incredible women throughout the years.

Joyce Thomas

Most of the stories in the last few chapters are at least a little humorous; at least I hope so. But this one is only meant to be full of love, admiration, and gratitude.

The week in 1970 our second son, 10-pound 3-ounce Patrick Richard (Rick), was about to be born was one of the luckiest weeks of our lives for two extraordinary reasons — one obviously personal and the other one having to do with business (and as it has turned out, personal too). First, of course, was the birth of Rick, four weeks late, on the day after Thanksgiving in 1970. My mother-in-law, a nurse, had come to help a week after our due date in 1970 and stayed two weeks more and then had to leave to go home as Rick still had not been born. Finally Rick did arrive to the joy of all. And our son, Jay, would have a little (big) brother.

The second blessing was that Joyce Thomas walked into our office at 2200 Palm Beach Lakes Boulevard. We had put an ad in the newspaper for part-time help as it was becoming obvious that with two babies under seventeen months, I was not going to be doing all that I had done in the past. Enter…Joyce Thomas, the indomitable Joyce Thomas. How could we possibly know, forty-five years later, she would still be at the helm every working day of the week (as well as some weekends), every week of the year with very, very few exceptions. I can count on one hand the number of days Joyce has called in sick out of about twelve thousand workdays. Maybe less than five sick days ever? I do not lie. In addition, Joyce, who has moved from part-time girl Friday to secretary to office manager, then part-time manager, then secretary of our corporate business, has been there nights and weekends whenever needed. We actually owe her about a year and a half of vacation time but she never takes it. She comes in at 8:15 a.m. every morning and she doesn't leave most of the time until 7:00 p.m. She is the most stable personality I've ever met. I'm always asking her if she is on "happy pills" because rarely is she anything but upbeat and delightful. There is no situation that Joyce cannot and does not handle, often multitasking while handling it. She represents us with grace and composure. She is as loyal and honest a friend and employee as I've ever met. She has been a confidant to John, Jay, and me. All the time…she amazes me. I call her Saint Joyce as I have yet to find anything in which I could ever fault her. She is/has been a blessing of incalculable value.

Thank you, Joyce! Your incredible work ethic has not gone unnoticed or unappreciated. I have no idea where Manero's would be without you. You are heaven sent and when we count our blessings, you are at the top of the list.

Delightful Idiosyncrasies of Restaurant People

Over the years we have had some of the most extraordinary people work with us to make our business successful. In addition we have had some of the craziest, wildest, most dysfunctional people that you could ever imagine.

Being one who always looks for the best in people, I always try to affirm the positive and work on the negative. No one of us is perfect, least of all me, and I'm sure any one of our employees and certainly my family could give you a handful or more of my personality traits which they would like to modify or maybe eliminate. When you are in our kind of business, employees as well as guests often become part of your family. You walk with them through good times and bad. The restaurant business is a microcosm of all of life. That being said, over the course of the years I have observed the following about restaurant people:

> Most of us are a little bit nuts.
> We work when everyone else plays therefore the outlaw in us must come out sometime.
> We celebrate our holidays early in the morning or late in the night on the day before or the day after everyone else, or never.
>
> We have eternal guilt for not spending enough time with our families.
> We attract strange as well as wonderful people around us.
> Many (of the younger and carefree among us) play while everyone else sleeps.
> We have this business in our bones.

Long ago, when I was about seventeen, I remember reading a fascinating book by Herman Wouk called *Don't Stop the Carnival*.[11] It since has been made into a Broadway play. It took place on a Caribbean island and it was a hysterical account of what actually happens in the lodging and dining business. At the time I thought it was wonderfully outrageous. Today I realize that the situations described with employees were mild compared to what I know. Over the years we have had many situations with employees, customers, and other restaurateurs, some about which I cannot even bring myself to write.

But a few of those include:

> The chef, who was invited to bring a spouse or partner to our company party, and who came with his chimpanzee. (That left many unanswered questions in coworkers' minds.)
>
> The hostess who showed up for work insisting that it was within her rights to wear a (ugly) hat while working.
>
> The chef whose mom called in saying her son was sick and had to take a few days off — not telling us that he was in the county jail.
>
> The local restaurateur who, seeing our parking lot full, had no compunction about sending his kids over to put flyers advertising his place on all of our customers' cars.
>
> The laundry lady who would put food from our freezers in the bushes while "maintaining" the property and then picked it up late at night after closing.
>
> A customer who had just come from his local club where he intended to have dinner. He reported to Jay that he wouldn't be eating there at the club again for when he asked for his spaghetti "al dente," the server came back and told them they were out of "al dente" sauce.
>
> The customer, who complained after I did the Heimlich technique on him (saving his life) saying that he was just recovering from broken ribs.

The endless sous chefs caught drinking beer in the coolers, laundry room, or restrooms (you young'uns must come up with more unique places).

The more commonplace things like the maintenance man who came in with his "health drink" every morning. (Having been a mother of four teenagers I have learned to be able to identify what is an "I have been drinking the night before" smell as opposed to an "I am still drinking" smell on one's breath.) After a few weeks, I sent him out to put up the flag one day, only to find his "health drink" filled with rum which I later found out was from our bar.

The bartender who was selling drugs and providing ladies of the evening at the bar.

The hostess who had a deal with one of the servers to get a certain percentage of his tips if she seated the big tippers in his section only.

The maintenance man, who whenever I asked him a question, would answer: "I would love to talk to you, boss, but I'm running late."

The employees who absolutely stated it was not they when we showed them a security tape of them stealing beer.

And then...one of our waiters, JGH, who recently asked if he could use my cover-up. Thinking of course, because it was raining outside, that he wanted my jacket to go to his car, I gave it to him. He looked shocked, laughed, and said: "Oh no, Donna, I mean your under-eye cover-up!"

Observations of a Reluctant Restaurateur

Here are a few things I've always wanted to share with guests and friends. These are my guidelines wherever I go:

1. Always check out the restrooms first.

2. Be careful at an all-you-can-eat restaurant. It's a great place to get rid of food.
3. Eat cautiously and selectively from a buffet.
4. Always trust your nose.
5. Treat reviews with questionable respect.
6. The outside is your first clue. Most of the time the outside says something about the inside. But…every once in a while you get surprised.
7. Never trust a dirty chef.
8. Ask the servers what they would eat. (One time a server told me all the things he would not eat at his restaurant. We had a glass of wine and left.)
9. Good food costs money — don't go for the cheapest restaurant advertised. If a restaurant's prices seem too good a deal, it's probably because they're trying to clean out coolers, use inexpensive frozen food, or they don't know any better and will soon be out of business.
10. A good place will back up their food. Everyone makes mistakes. All restaurants can serve a bad meal or have a bad night. Let them know and give them a second chance.
11. Ask the locals — they generally know where to find the best food.
12. If you're buying pizza expect pizza prices. If you're buying pasta expect pasta prices. If you're buying chicken, expect chicken prices. If you're buying steak, expect to spend some money for good steak. Steaks cost more than chicken; chicken costs more than pizza; pizza costs more than pasta. (You do not want to go out to eat with me; while everyone is enjoying the conversation, I am smiling and adding up in my head the food cost of each menu item to see if it's fair.)
13. Cleanliness speaks — someone cares. If you see a problem with the environment, let the management know.
14. Most restaurants don't survive the first year. Find one with a good track record, not a place that is in and out of business.
15. Researchers from UCLA tell us that we spend about fifty-two minutes preparing dinner at home every single night. So when

you dine out, use that time to enjoy the pleasure that is being provided to you. Slow down. Don't rush a good meal.

16. And finally, please...if you have a problem with your dining experience, let the management know *when* it happens, not on your way out the door when it's too late. We can't see everything, although we try. Good restaurants will go out of their way to make you happy and satisfied and will correct any problem, but first they must be made aware of it.

Remember, food is sacred. A good chef will put love into the cooking and a good restaurant will treat you as a valued guest at their table. Enjoy your experience whether you are sharing a meal with family or friends (or even eating alone). Put the smartphones away. No one is more important than the person in front of you. We want to make you happy and help you have a pleasure-filled time. Dining out should be at the top of the list of all human experiences. At Manero's, you should know...your satisfaction is always guaranteed.

Jay and me in the lobby at Manero's of Palm City.

Donna Tiernan Mahoney

Personal Reflections of a Reluctant Restaurateur

We craft Love from heartbreak, Compassion from shame,
Grace from disappointment, Courage from failure.
—Brene Brown

When we first opened the restaurant in Palm City, John had just died. His death was painful, frightening, and overwhelming. There was no good news but the experience was also transformative, in many ways. The philosopher, Paul Tillich, teaches that when you endure suffering of any kind, you are taken beneath the everyday realities of life and find that you are no longer the person you used to be. I found this to be so true in my own life, as unknown to many, my inner life was getting stronger every day. According to David Brooks, a columnist for the *New York Times*:

> The right response to this kind of pain is not pleasure. It's holiness. I don't even mean this in a purely religious sense. It means seeing life as a moral drama, placing the hard experiences in a moral context and trying to redeem bad by turning it into something sacred.[12]

This is how I felt when we opened our new venture in Palm City: Our kids had college degrees and beyond and could have done anything. They are all quite capable and three of our four children stepped up to the family plate with Jay running our new business in Palm City, Florida, and Rick and Erin running our Manero's, DBA J. Arthur's, in Maggie Valley, North Carolina. Our older daughter, Shannon, opened her law office in West Palm Beach — the only one to take John's and my advice to "get out of the restaurant business." But here I was, once again, back where I started in the restaurant many years ago, but now the eldest survivor and matriarch of the family business. Life indeed can be circuitous: a blessing and a curse.

But mostly…a blessing.

Since then, the blessings have been many. All of our kids married and have given us eight grandchildren. I share all of them with my new beloved husband, Tim, who has filled my life with joy and fun.

Friends say he's the anchor and I'm the sail. Boy do I value that anchor.

I have come to an understanding that, indeed, my dream of becoming a psychologist has been fulfilled along the road in more ways than I ever could have imagined. Often Dan Eldon's words: "The journey is the destination" come crashing down on me. "It's the journey, Donna," I keep telling myself. The wonder has been happening every single moment of every day. No longer am I waiting for that day that I become a psychologist. My life has been a school of psychology, rich with meaning and adventure and wonderful relationships every single day. What more could any person want?

In this crazy, mixed-up business, I've been able to connect with people at every juncture of their lives and use skills of ministry, psychology, social work, and hospitality as well as my restaurant, administration, and new culinary skills to comfort, entertain, empower, encourage, teach, console, and energize the people sent my way. Serving another person a meal is a truly sacred act. Offering food and drinks to another is a gift if done with love and hospitality. This gift I have been able to offer to many. In addition, I've received all these gifts back tenfold in a variety of ways from so many people, and mostly from my family, each of whom is extraordinary in his or her own way. As I approach the age at which many choose to retire, I am filled with energy, passion, and enthusiasm to see the next chapter for Manero's. It has been a fulfilling and exciting way to live a life up until now and I am very thankful.

So far, life has been different than what I had envisioned. I've been overwhelmed in endless ways with a "quality of fullness" by our laughing God.

I may have been *Seduced by Gorgonzola*, but oh…what a blessed event it has been.

All journeys have secret destinations of which the traveler is unaware.
—Martin Buber

CHAPTER SIX
Pilgrimage to Gorgonzola

The Trip There

I am writing this in the present tense as we are making the trip from Mougins, France, where we are staying for a week on our anniversary trip. The season has ended in Maggie Valley and the leaves are all off the trees. Business will be a lot less hectic now except for the snowy weekends and the upcoming holidays, so we have used this opportunity to get away.

Tim and I left our hotel in Mougins (pronounced Moo ja) this morning at about five o'clock to catch a 6:15 a.m. train from Cannes to Milan, Italy, where we will take the subway, train, or taxi for the approximately ten-kilometer trip from Milan to Gorgonzola, Italy. We are going to visit the site of the original place where the cheese that we use in our "world famous" Gorgonzola salad, was introduced to the world. I have been looking forward to this adventure and I know that it will have all my Manero ancestors dancing in the heavens. The fact that someone finally went back and paid tribute to the town that had

Seduced by Gorgonzola

such a part in providing for the family will keep them feasting at still another heavenly banquet of epicurean delights.

Each pulling a small suitcase, we arrive at the station earlier than needed as we didn't know what to expect with the local traffic. It was not a good idea to arrive this early as many of the unsavory characters in the area have also chosen to show up at the station before dawn. Or...perhaps they spent the entire night? I am not the nervous type, however, I am anxious about this situation. Tim reminds me to lighten up and think about the fact that most people would give their eyeteeth to be anywhere in Cannes, even at the train station. I feel guilty and I agree, but still, I am scared.

The train arrives at the station in Cannes on time and we find it, miraculously, with the help of the locals. In my estimation, the French show a lack of concern for tourists, being that they post absolutely nothing any place public in English, except for a few signs at the airport. We have found the only exception to be at restaurants and hotels where the owners want to attract customers. We board the train for the journey that will take us to Milan. The magnificent view takes my mind off the less than sanitary conditions on the train as we pass through many beautiful towns on the Mediterranean such as Antibes, Nice, Monte Carlo, and Menton, France and we travel toward the border and the Italian Riviera.

For much of this ride we see the ocean on our right. It is a blustery and rainy day. Regardless, it is spectacular. We have a short layover at the French/Italian border in Ventimiglia, Italy, before boarding our next train. Now I can use my Italian. I am psyched and think back to what *Signora Bellefiore* at Manhattanville, my Italian professor, originally from Milan, would think of me now. We use this time to purchase "una tazza de te," a cup of tea. The young girl looks at me like I'm nutzo, and then I repeat it in English. This she easily understands. I am positive I have pronounced it correctly and think to myself that she is probably Russian.

We have reserved seats on the next train, learning years ago in Italy when we got in some trouble by sitting in the wrong seats, that on Trenitalia one must have tickets *and* reserved seats. When we get on the train we think we are going to have the six-seat cabin all to ourselves so we spread out a little, but within one stop the train is filled to capacity. Each stop when someone gets off we think again that we will have some privacy but soon realize this is not to be as repeatedly people come and go with their mozzarella and onion or pastrami and garlic sandwiches, making the cabin smell like an Italian deli. We too have brought our sandwiches, ham and cheese, knowing the train would not have a dining car, but at least we were thoughtful enough not to make them with strong deli smells. The ticket seller looked at me like I was crazy when I asked about a dining car and I was reminded of my mom who would say in her Italian dialect: "Tu sei pozza?" Mom translated this as "Are you crazy?"

When we arrive at the station in Milan, it is about 12:45 p.m. I repeatedly ask, in my first year Italian, where we can get some information. The Milan station is nothing short of a noisy maze. I have researched the train to Gorgonzola on the internet. I am sure one used to run there but couldn't quite figure out if it was still running out that far from Milan. We are in need of a little bit of direction. We finally get to the bottom floor after walking around following confusing signs on all three stories (the Italians could really use a little help from the Germans here). The signs are directing us to the information station but we find out that there really is no information desk, only ticket sellers. We are told to take a number and wait. This is troublesome as all we want to find out is *if* the train still runs there. If it doesn't, we will move on to plan B. Our ticket number is #189 and the number on the board says #107. A German lady with number #141 comes up to the attendant who was handing out the numbers and screams in her broken English that she has been waiting for thirty-five minutes and it looks like she still has twenty-five more to go. She is irate. By my calculations that's putting us in the ticket seller's window in about an hour and twenty-five minutes.

In the meantime, a questionable-looking young man comes up to Tim and indicates that he could help us. I tell Tim that the young man is not identified as a station attendant and that he should not listen to him. Tim and I have this little discussion (some may call it an argument) in the middle of the station. Tim tells me I'm paranoid and that this man can help us. I tell him he is extremely naïve (he, always expecting the best in people, is thinking that all young Italians belong to the Italian Christian Youth Group) and I think that this guy just wants him to take his wallet out and be off with it. Having had that happen once in Rome I'm aware of "mi cugini" propensity to pickpocket, especially in places like train stations. We discussed the matter back and forth before I finally convince him (for the sake of the marriage) to follow me so that we can go and get a cab. The €35-€50 ride will be well worth it not to put up with this situation in the station any longer.

We find a taxi outside the large station and a (seemingly) pleasant taxi driver tells us by his facial expression that he would be happy to take us to Gorgonzola but he needs the address. Address? All I have is the name "Hotel Senator" in the Expedia confirmation. I had assumed from what I have read that Gorgonzola is so small there is probably only one street running through town (look it up on the internet and check it out on the webcam). The Trip Advisor reviews state that there is very little to do in Gorgonzola, so I am expecting nothing but some cheese factories and a few churches.

The streets of Milan are beyond noisy and wild, making New York City look like Fiji by comparison. I ask the cab driver, in my best Italian, if he can put it into his GPS and he responds: "GPS?" I then ask him if he has his phone as my "global plan" which I arranged for back in the States has not yet been the least bit helpful in Europe. He says, unbelievably, "no telefono" and we say "grazie" and once again I look at Tim, and we begin to pull the luggage back into the station. I get out my jetpack which will allow us to have internet access so we can find the address of the hotel and return to the cab area. We find a nice, brightly lit McDonald's which makes my heart leap for joy as I'm thinking it will be safe and clean. We can take a seat in the back of the large establishment where I can open the tablet and get online with the jetpack. We sit ourselves down and I try with no luck. I then try my smartphone, still with no internet access.

Tim sees two lovely young Italian girls sitting next to us and asks them: "Speaka English?" One of them tells us "yes" and that she would be happy to help us. She puts the Hotel Senator into her phone but has no luck. She then tells us she will go outside where, she thinks, the internet can be accessed. She returns and gives us the address and then we strike up a conversation, being extremely grateful for this small (but large to us) favor. She tells us she is planning to go to New York City to become a dancer. The girls are both delightful and helpful and we offer to buy them something else but they graciously decline. We then give them our business cards and tell them if we can ever help them when they come to the United States (as if the U.S. is the size of Maggie Valley) to give us a call. "Arrivederci," we say and "grazie."

We have the address and proceed back to the taxi area. While we were in McDonald's a crowd of about two hundred Muslim men gathered near the cab stand to protest and are yelling loudly and all holding signs which read in Italian "morte di Aasad" which I translate as "death to Assad." When I see the signs and see the fifty or more Italian policemen with their uzis, all I want is the safety of any Italian taxi driver, even on who might cause us to ride with our stomachs in our mouth. Unfortunately, that's the cabbie we get but I say about ten Hail Mary's and decided to "let go and let God," wondering if the life insurance payment I made was received before I left the United States and hoping to God that that She or He will get us to the Hotel Senator after all. Finally after about twenty minutes we pull into this lovely hotel in the District of Gorgonzola.

Kiss the Ground: We're In Gorgonzola, Italy

We are really here. It is about 3:00 p.m. The weather is inclement: pouring rain, dark, and windy but I don't care. We have achieved part one of the goal and nothing will stop us from getting our pictures. No matter what happens to us now my Manero ancestors will know that Tim and Donna made the pilgrimage to Gorgonzola. We are finally here. I get out of the cab and throw air kisses to the ground.

By my calculations, we have about two hours of daylight in Gorgonzola on this first day and we will have about another six hours tomorrow before we have to take a taxi back to Milan. What we are not sure of is if the rain and wind will continue all through our time here, so Tim and I both agree, he being from Ireland where it rains eighty percent of the time, that as bad as the weather is today it could be worse tomorrow. (This is an Irish maxim.) Then we ask about a taxi and the woman at the desk tells us there are not a lot of them in Gorgonzola and that we will do better to start to walk in the rain. So we agree to put on our warm clothes, get our mini umbrellas, and begin the ten-minute walk into the town of Gorgonzola.

We're in Gorgonzola!

We start out on the little footpath. As soon as we see the first sign that reads "Gorgonzola," I implore Tim to take pictures with both the phone camera and my tablet. The weather is abominable but we came here to get pictures and see the place and who knows if it will be worse in the morning. Tim, a saint of a man (this expression is used in Ireland to describe any man who is tied up with a somewhat challenging woman) obliges by taking pictures of me by every possible sign we see. (This really touches my heart and increases my love for Tim as he has always told me that he is sure that he will die of a death by rain, as he claims many of his ancestors did.) It is pouring cats and dogs but as we walk the entire town, we are still able to see the churches and the many shops and storefronts. Within a half-hour, it is quite dark but we have taken a picture of every sign visible and finally decide to warm up and get dry. Luckily, we find an adorable little café, Via Lattés Café. We stop in to get some wine and appetizers. It was a great decision.

Tim, an Irish ambassador of sorts, is probably about the most gregarious person one could ever meet. He talks to everyone whether they want to listen or not. One cannot escape his rhetoric. And so he begins to talk to the people at a nearby table in this lovely little café as he recognizes that one is, providentially, speaking English and the other, Italian. We sit, noshing our food, while trying to figure out their relationship. We figure they are a couple and invite them to our table. We ask if we can buy them a glass of wine and the woman, who we later came to know as Catarina, laughs and says: "Oh no, I own the place." She asks us to call her Cate and then directs her eyes and nods to her husband, "Gaetano," who is behind the counter working with her young handsome son. The conversation continues and as the other guests come and go, it gets livelier and livelier. The English speaker is a young au pair, Aaron, from Liverpool, who stops in the café frequently to help Cate. He is trying to teach Cate English and at the same time he is trying to become more fluent in Italian. We spend about an hour with them, enjoying light conversation, picking up a little local color and finally, we ask Cate to recommend a good restaurant for dinner. This she does. We take pictures promising to email and perhaps to stop in again tomorrow. We love to make new friends and we have had so many laughs in this place. The whole hour-long interaction is delightful and regardless of whatever else happens, we are thrilled so far about our trip to Gorgonzola. We have long forgotten the frustrating time we had getting from the station to the hotel.

By the time we returned to the Hotel Senator the weather has deteriorated and we decide that rather than take Cate's recommendation, we will go out to a fancy-looking restaurant across the street. I suppose the restaurant was located there because of the hotel and the business community that surrounds it. When we enter, we recognize that the place is full of young Polish males, all, I am sure, on hefty expense accounts. The restaurant is expensive, stuffy, has terrible service, and is not particularly good. We eat our lamb cutlets, pay our hundred plus euro bill and return to the hotel, upset with ourselves that we did not take Cate's suggestion but happy with our beautiful warm room where we can get a good night's sleep.

The next day we awake to thunder, lightning, more rain, and gusty winds. After a beautiful breakfast at the hotel, the concierge tells us we can use the hotel's umbrellas to make the ten-minute trip to town. We thought the weather had calmed down a little and that the lightning had stopped. However, after taking our first twenty steps from the front door our big umbrellas, which the concierge has loaned us, turn inside out, making us look like Mary Poppins a-flight. We realize now that walking is not a good idea. We come back to the lobby and ask for a taxi to be called. The concierge, a different one, tells us that it will be about fifteen minutes and that there are not a lot of taxis in Gorgonzola, confirming what we heard yesterday. We wait and wait and soon a nice-looking van shows up with the name Fascination on it. Apparently, the only taxi in town also serves as a van for the owner's travel agency. The driver speaks fluent English and for the short ride around town, he fills our heads with facts and information. Our driver, in addition to driving the taxi and owning the travel agency, has also been an international electrical engineer, which is why he speaks English so well. Incredibly, he tells us that he is also the organizer (and I understand him to say that he was also the initiator) of the annual Gorgonzola Festival that takes place for three days every year on the last weekend in September. I am stunned by this coincidence/miracle of fate that we should end up, without even requesting it, being driven around town by the initiator of this incredible festival. He drives slowly, as requested, and we take a few pictures as we continue asking questions, and he, delightedly, gives us information. One picture we take is of what could have been a Gorgonzola cheese headquarters in earlier years. I'm delighted with this picture because I know it will help us in the cheesy story we will one day tell. We tell him why we are here and a little about ourselves as he drives us past the two churches which delight Tim to no end. After flying across the ocean, arriving in France and making this adventuresome train trip to Gorgonzola, known as the home of the cheese that made the Manero family famous, I decide to ask this fount of information about the locations of all the cheese factories.

I'm brought face-to-face with the sad truth as told to me by the organizer of the Gorgonzola Festival, as he decides to drop the bomb. He tells us, quite apologetically: "Well…Gorgonzola is not made in Gorgonzola, Italy." I questioned his statement. He repeats, "Yes…it is true. Gorgonzola is not made in Gorgonzola, and in fact, there is little evidence, only legends, to substantiate that it was ever made here." I had read rumors that the cheese was not currently made here and that would have been okay. But now I am being told that the authenticity of the home place of Gorgonzola cheese is questioned and perhaps it was never made here. "Send in the clowns," I think to myself. This possibility was suggested on the internet as some of the local towns are constantly arguing some of these facts. Now I'm getting it from one who has lived here all his life. He knows. And what he knows is that we shall never know. Some say it originated here as far back as the thirteenth century. Others claim they can trace it back to the year 879 in Gorgonzola. But nothing can really be known for sure. All we do know is that today it is made in the Lombardy and Piedmont regions.

I am chastened and humbled.

The van driver/travel agent/electrical engineer/festival organizer (this is the type of person I can relate to) drops us off, dejected, but still we are going to find some way to pull this out of the fiasco that it is. All our family and friends know about this trip and that we planned to come here and the reason why. It was to be somewhat of an epicurean pilgrimage. I've made many pilgrimages in my lifetime in the spiritual or religious sphere but this was different. And now…

We proceed around town in the rain. The buildings are a little protection from the wind so we continue stopping inside one large duomo and then a small chiesa for consolation. Both are lovely in their own ways. (This part of the journey is pleasing Tim to no end, making me think of Dad who claimed that my mom dragged him into every church on the European continent when they traveled there.)

We continue to make our way to the park where we take several pictures as the rain has subsided temporarily. We stop in at the tabbacceria and once again a young girl who is serving our table does not understand my perfect Italian. "Vorrei una coke e un aqua," I say. Once again, I get a blank stare and I say it again, but louder. By this time, all twelve of the Italian men in the little shop look at me, thinking "dumb American" and finally I get up, go to the bar, and point to the two requests. I just don't understand why Italian is not spoken in Italy. We get a can of Coke for which we are charged four euros or $5.50, and the water for which we are charged three euros. Tim says they must've seen us coming.

We have promised our wonderful and talented Chef Cedric (now Tim's best friend as Cedric used to work in Kilkenny, Ireland, the town where Tim went to seminary) at Bistro 21 back in our hotel in Mougins that we will bring him back some Gorgonzola from its birthplace. Now, however, it has become apparent to us, especially when we walk into the cheese shop, that to bring Gorgonzola from here is ridiculous. Heck, it's not even produced here. It would be just as easy to get it in Cannes rather than bringing the delicious but pungent cheese into our cabin on the train and stink up the cabin like everyone else does.

We continue our walk around town and end up back at Cate and Gaetano's café where we have lunch and a final glass of wine before walking back to the hotel to get back to Milan. We discuss the Gorgonzola situation with Cate who said she knew, but she would never have said it (like this is a big plot directed at crazy Gorgonzola cheese aficionados). Regardless, I love her already and forgive her. We say our goodbyes and head back to the hotel to gather our luggage for the short trip to the Milan station.

The Return from Gorgonzola

Since the only taxi person in Gorgonzola is now busy selling trips to Miami to Italians, a Bentley limo shows up to return us to the station. It is immaculate, smells fresh and leathery and the driver is a good one. Apparently this is a vehicle that transports the Samsung officials back and forth to the airport and station and we were able to get it while it wasn't busy. When we get out the driver asks us if €50 ($68) is all right for the 6-mile journey and we readily agree. It would be worth anything to get us safely back inside the station and onto the train. We say "ciao, grazie" and make our way to the station for the 3:00 p.m. trip back to Cannes.

We find our train and make our way to our cabin, convincing ourselves that we will be the only ones there, but little by little, four other people wind their way in. We have the two seats in the middle facing each other. I begin my book, *Wonder*, (which I highly recommend to every person age eleven or older) and Tim returns to his book. Darkness descends and the garlic and onion sandwiches come out from people's bags, but we concentrate on our reading. The train runs late all along and the Italian women and men, to the left and right of us discuss in loud and exaggerated voices with wild hand movements how frustrated they are with Trenitalia. We smile and nod our heads, trying not to look like *The Ugly Americans*. Other than that, the trip on this train is uneventful and we finally make it to the Ventimiglia station.

We catch the next train to Cannes. This French train has open seating and we notice several young men take over our car. They must've been traveling for several days as the odor in the train was overwhelming. The train leaves the station and within no time we are in Monaco, France. At the Monaco station, several police come aboard to check either the passports or the tickets. Their numbers are a little frightening. We never find out if they were checking passports or tickets since we aren't checked but several of these young men are. They are all escorted from the train to God knows where and there are just five of us left when the police leave our car. The ousted young men seem to be of Eastern European origin, perhaps Bulgarian or Romanian. I feel sorry for them as they didn't seem to be bothering anyone, but today everyone is suspect.

With all that is going on in the world and the bias against Americans, not to mention the fears of Ebola, this trip was thought by some of our family not to be prudent. Tim and I agree that life is meant to be lived boldly. In spite of that, we are conscious of these happenings and try to keep ourselves aware of our surroundings. As we pull out of Monaco, the train picks up speed but within five minutes begins to slow. As it does we hear a bloodcurdling scream scaring us to the point that all five of us put our heads in our laps thinking it is a terrorist attack. I think back to the warnings of family and friends and a wave of fear runs

Seduced by Gorgonzola

through me. The scream seems to be moving as if someone is running from car to car. The scream continues incessantly for what seems like about five minutes although it was probably two or three. Finally, a policewoman comes running through and tells us that it is okay. We find out that someone's luggage was stolen and the guy who stole it jumped out of the train while it was still running. The gentleman whose luggage is stolen is understandably irate and literally screams at another policewoman all the way back to the next station. A French man sitting close to us tells us he takes this train every night and that situations of this nature happen frequently.

"Enough," I say to myself. Let's get back to our hotel room. Finally the train arrives in Cannes at 11:00 p.m. Tim has already visited the men's room on the last train and decides not to risk it again. We gather our things and head for our car. Tim needs to use the restroom again but they are all locked up so he has to wait. Thank God, I am thinking, because the station has no police presence and the many questionable-looking characters who were here yesterday morning in addition to some more street people are gathering. We make our way in the dark up the hundred steps toward the car but not before paying our parking fee, which turns out to be €205 or about $270 at that time. (We always seem to plan our trips when the euro value is up.) We look at each other, tired and upset with ourselves that we did not park in the garage, which we had decided against for safety reasons. We blame the French and the fact that there are no English-speaking signs in the French Riviera. Had we known there was a $200 difference in price we would have parked in the enclosed parking lot rather than leave it out in the open. Still, I say to Tim, it has been worth it.

Tim puts our credit card in the machine, while I am scanning the area all around us in the shadows, knowing men have little peripheral vision. We go to the car, lock ourselves in, and proceed to leave the parking area. After touring the town of Mougins in the dark, as we are slightly lost, we arrive back at our hotel room after midnight, having safely made our trip to Gorgonzola with both phone camera and tablet in hand. Between the camera and tablet, we have about hundred pictures from Gorgonzola in our possession. These are our prized possessions. I plan to sleep with the camera and tablet next to the bed in case we are broken into during the night. Take anything you want but not our pictures. As we continue to find our way to our temporary home, I could not help but wonder what Mama Mia Ellen Manero Tiernan, who used to say "Donna doesn't want to miss anything in life" would think of her offspring.

Tim and me celebrating the joy of our trip.

We get back to our suite on the lovely grounds of Le Club Mougins, open the door, lock it on the inside and give each other a rollicking hug and kiss. We go to the kitchen, make ourselves pasta, and pour a couple of glasses of wine. I think of the words of Ruth Reichl: "Pull up a chair. Take a taste. Come join us. Life is endlessly delicious." We are wide awake now, safe, warm, dry, together, and excited by our romantic adventure to Milan and Gorgonzola. We mull over the experiences of the last two days and laugh until we cry. We are thrilled that we just made an overnight trip costing well over €1400 to a place that in reality was somewhat of a hoax. Regardless, what a wonderful forty-four hours of our lives. Life, indeed, is good.

Once again, we have been seduced by Gorgonzola.

And once again, what an exciting, irresistible, and fun-filled seduction it was.

Restaurant Information

To the best of my knowledge the following businesses have been under the Manero's influence, however, I do not suggest that this is an inclusive list:

> Nick Manero and his flagship Manero's in Greenwich owned and/or franchised the following:
> Syosset, New York
> Manhasset, New York
> Roslyn, New York
> Long Beach, Long Island, New York
> Hartsdale, New York
> Stony Point, New York
> Poughkeepsie, New York
> 34th Street in New York City

Manero's in Paramus, New Jersey, was franchised to Dan Dowd, not a relative.

My mom and dad with Uncle Nick originally owned and operated Manero's in Hallandale and until 1986, owned Manero's in West Palm Beach.

After Nick Sr.'s death, Manero's in Greenwich and eventually in Hallandale were owned and operated by my cousin, Nick Manero.

Porky (Clarence Manero) had Manero's in Orange and Manero's in Westport. According to my cousin, Mary Manero, he also had a Porky Manero's on Route 128 in Massachusetts. Manero's on the Berlin Turnpike, this one, operated by Porky's stepson, Jack Wells, from his first marriage to Betty, was (reportedly) a joint venture. He also operated his 19th Hole Nightclub on Steamboat Road in Greenwich in the '30s and '40s.

Tony Manero owned and operated a restaurant in the Riverside/Cos Cob area in the early '50s.

Mention is also made in newspaper articles about a Manero's in Secaucus, New Jersey owned by the Manero brothers. I am not sure of the accuracy of these reports.

My brother Peter owned and operated a Manero's in Margate, Florida.

John and I operated and then bought Manero's in West Palm Beach, owned and operated Martha's Kitchen, and J. Arthur's Restaurant in Maggie Valley, North Carolina and were the exclusive caterer to the Atlanta Braves in South Florida for many years. John was the mastermind behind the plans for Manero's in Palm City.

The Mahoney Family at the wedding of Shannon Mahoney and John Whittles, 2011.
Left to right, adults: Rick and Michelle Mahoney, Tim Lynch and Donna Mahoney Lynch, Shannon (Mahoney) and John Whittles, Erin (Mahoney) and Frank Varvoutis, Jay and Marcy Mahoney.
Children: Keagan, Reilly, and John Patrick Mahoney, Isabella and Lillie Varvoutis, Jake and Matthew (front) Mahoney.
Courtesy of Shannon Mahoney Whittles and John Whittles.

Seduced by Gorgonzola

The fourth generation of Maria Grace and Giovanni Mainiero's offspring would be my kids, as well as many other great grandchildren and cousins. Research shows approximately twelve percent of family businesses survive into the third generation and only three percent into the fourth. I am proud that we are in those numbers. The three family members who remain in the day-to-day operations of the business, Jay, Rick, and Erin (Shannon advises) each have their own unique style and characteristics of Manero, Tiernan, and Mahoney in them, making them well equipped to deal with any task on their plate. Like Eleanor Roosevelt, the words, "can't be done" are not in their mindset. If there is a restaurant challenge, they will figure out a way to handle it with the expertise that would make all the restaurateurs before us very proud.

Today our family owns and operates Manero's in Palm City, and J. Arthur's in Maggie Valley. Under our family corporation we have operated or currently operate two country clubs, a large concession in Stuart, a food van and food operations at a gun club in Palm City. We have provided catering for up to 1300 people and we have online internet sales. Having just successfully come through the worst business cycle in any of our restaurants' histories, we are looking forward to what is ahead. After all, the fifth generation is just around the corner.

The fifth generation, minus baby Ella.
John Patrick, Jake, Reilly,
Keagan, Isabella, Matthew, and Lillie.

For every one of these endeavors I have heard hundreds of stories over the years with incredible emotion, memory, and feeling. The Manero name has struck a chord with millions of diners over the decades. The seduction of Gorgonzola has impacted many others as well. Only a few of them could be related in this book.

Maria Gracia Marantony
c 1876-1954

The Mainiero Family
Three Generations

Giovanni Marantony
c 1875 - c 1934

Mary 1896-1986
m
John Margenot

Albert d
Carl d
Vera d
John

Nicholas 1904-1980
m
Frances Murphy

Carmelita d
Nicholas Jr.

Clarence 1906-1970
m
Florence Taylor

Angelina 1908-1961
m
Dominic Costaugni

George
Danny d
John

Jackie 1909-1927

Ellen 1912-2001
m
James Arthur Tiernan

Donna
Peter

Agnes 1914-2003
m
Tony Manero

Richard
Robert d

Rosine 1918-1991
m
Joseph Bohacs

The Manero Family
Three Generations

Donna - 1947
α
John Mahoney
(d-1998)

John
α
Narcy Stephens

John Jacob
Matthew

Patrick
α
Michelle Seman

John Patrick
Reilly
Kagan

Ellen Marion Mainiero
1912 - 2001

Shannon
α
John Whittles

Ella

Erin
α
Frank Varacutes

Lillie
Isabella

The Tiernan Family - est 1940
Four Generations

James Arthur Tiernan
1915 - 2006

January
α
Jason Gatto

Peter - 1949
α
Beverly Nickland

Peter
α
Emily Guys

James

The Tiernan Family
Four Generations

ACKNOWLEDGMENTS

In writing a book, one recognizes the wide variety of people that have taken the book into its final form. Those people may range from the person who first suggested that one might have something to say, the one who kept the house clean so that the writer could do her work, the ones who did research for her, to the ones who helped get it to press, and a whole variety of people in between, too many to be acknowledged, but to whom the author is grateful.

So I begin the arduous task of trying to include the many people who have been godsends to me in this effort:

To the many customers across the years who have shared with me so many stories filled with memories and meaning, I thank you.

My cousins, Mary Manero (spouse of Robert, RIP), Ginny and John Costaregni, George and Lillian Costaregni, and Susie Costaregni, all of whom live in the Greenwich area have been invaluable to me in providing family information both from their memories and from local resources. Thank you for all your help in researching our family's background, much with which I was unfamiliar. A special thank you to the above mentioned Costaregnis who also directed me to my Aunt Mary's book (chapter one), which was an invaluable resource. Thank you also to Rose Costaregni and Dan and Beth Costaregni for your approval on the story of your husband and dad, Danny.

The research librarian at Greenwich library, Carl White, took the time to return my call, and gather some articles from microfilm. Thank you, Carl.

Nola Taylor of the Greenwich Historical Society was extremely helpful and unrelenting in researching information, especially about The 19th Hole and correcting information that had been distorted in many articles which have been written. Thank you, Nola!

Many wrote letters and sent me information and in particular, Bill Masucci, Mary Jo Nataline Skarsgard, and Rich Rainey. Thanks to each of you for taking the time to send your loving and kind words. And to close friends, Patricia Pavelka, beloved friend from my childhood, and Emilio Diamantis, Jack Scarola, Esq., and Tom Roberts who shared so much of life with us ever since the West Palm Beach years and helped made it beautiful, thank you.

Martha Heimbach is my lifelong friend, who ran Martha's Kitchen and had the guts and stamina to write about it. What a blessed day it was when she walked into our first home. My love and admiration is eternal for you, Martha.

To my brother, Peter, a brilliant legal author, who helped me remember many of the stories of our childhood and my sister-in-law, B. J. Tiernan, herself an author (I suggest her *Standing on a Whale*, a great read) who guided me in the publishing process: thank you both for your love and support. Both of you are such a gift in my life. My nephew, Peter Tiernan, teacher of literature, encouraged me not to rush, to take my time and do a good job, and his lovely spouse, Emily, helped me navigate the blog process. I am so grateful. My niece, January Tiernan Gatto, who has also done research on Manero's, shared information provided to her by past staff members. I thank you, Jan.

Marnie Poncy, loving life-sister, who, after reading the manuscript, helped me refine the title and wrote the forward. Thank you, Marnie, for being a fortress of love, humor, and strength during so many challenges.

Rich Gays is my lifelong friend and was a confidant of my dad. To him I am so grateful for all his contributions of stories and many sessions of laughter. May they continue. I love you, Rich.

Joyce Thomas, the unsinkable, has been with the Manero's team for forty-five years. I cannot say enough about my admiration and awe of her. Thank you, Joyce, for your input with your stories as well as your loyalty, patience, and customer care over the years.

To Diana (Dee) Vitullo-Grover, my college roommate, well-loved friend of many years and editor who took my long and confusing sentences and family relationships and made sense of them. I am eternally grateful, Dee.

Marilyn Melfi and her recently deceased, delightful husband, Al, who, sadly, passed away during this endeavor, started out as customers and became trusted and much-loved friends. Marilyn has been a mentor, encourager, supporter, and editor/publicist. Thank you for you unwavering support at all times of the day and night.

I owe great thanks to Joyce M. Gilmour who did the line editing for this process; she was made known to me by my dear friend and author, Father Ron Camarda, late in this project. Thank you for your tireless work and for educating me on details long forgotten. And to Ron, one of my readers who shared many meaningful seminary classes and life discussions: you are such a gift and I am so blessed to find you again.

My surprise visitor and focus of the story segment, "Hope Springs Eternal," *Ken*, reinforced my faith in God and increased my joy and tears immeasurably when he walked through my door and stayed for three hours the day before this book went to the publisher for its final editing. He had been in recovery for almost two years and looked incredibly good and healthy. He was in a positive relationship, which included children about whom he was crazy. He was doing well in his work and about to buy a home. He gave me his total permission and encouragement in writing his story of rebirth, although I did tell him I would change his name. Thank you, Ken. Belief in a person is a powerful transformer. In the seminary, my friend, Jerry, now Fr. Jerry Kaywell, who ministers on the West Coast of Florida, used to say: "It may not have been a miracle, but it was certainly more than a coincidence. It was a God-incident." Indeed, it was.

To my family, previously acknowledged, all of whom make this book possible, thank you for your love and support. I love you like crazy into eternity.

And finally, to my beloved Tim, who has supported, challenged, encouraged, strengthened, mentored, and loved me through this project and who has also provided me with hot delicious breakfasts, which I have enjoyed over the past two years while writing at the kitchen counter in the early mornings: You, Tim, show me the face of God and are my life-line in every way possible.

ENDNOTES

1. Greenwich, Connecticut Historical Society. I am grateful to Nola Taylor, researcher at the Greenwich Historical Society who researched and provided me all the information about Clarence Manero's ownership of The 19th Hole in Greenwich.
2. Rich Rainey gave me this information by calling Sedgefield Country Club, and finding Tony Manero's name and dates on a plaque on the wall.
3. Eileen Harrington, *An Enterprising Woman: Oral History Interview with Mary Mainiero Margenot* (Greenwich, CT: Friends of the Greenwich Library Oral History Project, 1986).
4. Three newspaper articles in my possession state this information, one from 1926 with Porky's picture, one from Bermuda years in the early '40s, and his obituary. However, the newspaper names are not included in the family history books.
5. Harrington, 41-42.
6. Connecticut Land Record Stats, 1953.
7. Robert Blair Kaiser, *Clerical Error* (New York: Continuum, 2002), 16-60.
8. Robert Blair Kaiser, *RFK Must Die* (New York: Overlook Press, 2008).
9. Donna Tiernan Mahoney, *Touching the Face of God* (Boca Raton: Jeremiah Press, 1991, published simultaneously in Cork, Ireland: Mercier Press, 1991). This is a more readable version of my master's degree, urging the Church to look at some of its outdated practices. It was published both in the States and in Ireland, and had, at least, the effect of getting a few people to think.

10 Ann Carnahan, *Nick Manero's Cook-Out Barbecue Book,* (New York: Arco Publishing Company, 1962), 84. Over the years, this recipe has been altered.
11 Herman Wouk, *Don't Stop the Carnival* (New York, Back Bay Books, 1965).
12 David Brooks, "Transformed by Ordeals," *Palm Beach Post,* April 9, 2014, A9.

Donna may be contacted at:
SeducedByGorgonzola.com
Donnamahoneyauthor.com
Facebook.com: Seduced by Gorgonzola